MONTANA'S
Bob Marshall Country

Bob Marshall • Scapegoat • Great Bear
Wilderness Areas & Surrounding Wildlands

Rick and Susie Graetz

REVISED EDITION 2004
First Edition published in 1985

Contributing writers
Dave Alt, Bob Cooney, Jim Posewitz, US Forest Service

Contributing photographers
Carr Clifton, Bob Cooney, Bill Cunningham, Douglass Dye, Bill Lancaster, Gus Wolfe

©2004 Northern Rockies Publishing
Rick and Susie Graetz
P.O. Box 1707, Helena, Montana 59624
thisismontana@aol.com

Book design by GingerBee Creative, Helena, Montana

All color and prepress work done in Montana, U.S.A.
Printed in Korea
ISBN 1-891152-4

Front Cover: The Chinese Wall. LARRY MAYER
Back Cover: *Todd Graetz on the South Fork of the Sun River Trail.* RICK AND SUSIE GRAETZ
Above: *The Valley of the North Fork of the Sun and Slategoat Mountain.* RICK AND SUSIE GRAETZ

THE BOB IN PERSPECTIVE

Published in 1985, the first edition of this work came from myriad notes and photos assembled during more than 15 years of trekking and skiing in excess of 2,000 miles of trails and ascending countless mountain summits in Bob Marshall country. I was a kid when we first started, and in that era of my life, long trail distances and *"bagging"* peaks was part of living. We moved fast and memories were stored for future story telling.

With the exception of an occasional walk in the periphery of the Bob, especially the Rocky Mountain Front, the Beartooth and other mountain wildlands in Montana and beyond took me away from this piece of the Northern Rockies for many years. The Bob Marshall became just a part of many great untrammeled places.

Susie and I returned in this summer of 2004 for a seven-day reunion trip with Bill Cunningham, a long-time backcountry companion, and several other friends with whom I had spent many days and nights in this fabled place. We hiked about 60 miles of the headwaters of both the Middle Fork of the Flathead and North Fork of the Sun. A week later, Susie and I again found ourselves heading into the Bob, this time with Mike Munoz — District Ranger of the Rocky Mountain Ranger station, Kraig Lang — the Wilderness Ranger, and Pat McGuffin and Dave Watts of the Montana Wilderness Association. The task was to look closely at the landscape for the proper photograph for a poster commemorating the 40th Anniversary of the 1964 enactment of the Wilderness Act — legislation that gave lasting protection to places like the Bob Marshall. We chose the Chinese Wall as our primary destination.

These two expeditions allowed ample time to observe the wilderness from a different perception. Many miles over many years clouds one's definition. As we passed through deep woods, areas changed by fire since previous visits, surveyed the beginnings of two storied rivers, crossed several passes and paralleled one of the great symbols of the Bob … the 13-mile-long Chinese Wall, no longer goal or summit oriented, I now looked at this place as a whole. And a couple of weeks after our second trek, a flight over a wide swath of this wilderness complex — courtesy of Ted Cogswell and Doug Forest — helped tie it all together. Susie and I have been extremely lucky to visit much of this planet's most incredible mountain sites. In our opinion, the Bob Marshall country rises above it all. It has only taken me 30 years to come to that realization.

This, the crown jewel of the nation's wilderness system, has it all. It's accessible and it's plenty big. The three contiguous Wilderness areas, the Bob Marshall, Scapegoat and Great Bear and surrounding de facto wilderness comprise 2.5 million acres. That's a piece of geography larger than some eastern states. In an inventory roll call, all the ingredients are here. The Bob is a magnificent gathering of soaring rocky peaks, shining snowfields, reefs, buttes, stately expanses of timber, park-like valleys and meadows, tranquil lakes, meandering flows, raucous whitewater and icy springs so pure that to sip it other than flat on your belly with your lips to the source is a sacrilege. The wildlife includes all-stars of the wild … grizzlies, black bear, wolves, elk, mountain lion, beaver, moose, wolverines and eagles. As an added attribute the Continental Divide, sending waters to the Missouri from its east flank, and to the Columbia from the windward aspect, gives it its backbone.

The human factor then provides another dimension. The aura of those who came before resonates in the cathedral hush of this place and casts an air of wonderment and respect. Legends from the past give life to many a trail and landmark. Time and space go well here!

So with this recognition and new-found awareness at hand, we present a revised edition — having kept, though, and left unedited, much of the original writing, especially words penned by men who saw the early days of this wilderness first hand. New photography has been added, as have additional chapters and thoughts. And again we froze son Todd in time on the back cover.

Read this missive, and then head out into the landscape on foot or by *"wilderness sport's car"* — the four-legged model, namely horseback. Montana's Bob Marshall country is your place … you own it … go explore it!

RICK GRAETZ
September 4, 2004
Jim & Chris Scott's Place
Yellow Bay, Flathead Lake, Montana

Top: 8,401-foot Crown Mountain and Scapegoat Mountain.   RICK AND SUSIE GRAETZ
Bottom: Looking at Red Butte from the south end of the Chinese Wall below Cliff Mountain.   RICK AND SUSIE GRAETZ

Top: Big George Gulch on the Rocky Mountain Front.   RICK AND SUSIE GRAETZ
Bottom: Haystack Butte on the Rocky Mountain Front west of Augusta.   RICK AND SUSIE GRAETZ

Top: *Below the west side of Headquarters Pass.*   RICK AND SUSIE GRAETZ
Bottom: *The Rocky Mountain Front looking toward Sawtooth and the North Fork of the Sun River country.*   RICK AND SUSIE GRAETZ

Top: Hannan Gulch.   BILL LANCASTER
Bottom: Yvon Chounard and Rick Ridgeway, fishing the North Fork of the Sun River.   RICK AND SUSIE GRAETZ

Kraig Lang and Mike Munoz descending the east side of Headquarters Pass.   RICK AND SUSIE GRAETZ

CONTENTS

THIS IS BOB MARSHALL COUNTRY
by Rick Graetz

With the temperature hovering at 30 degrees below zero and the wind-driven snow piled high, my climbing partner and I were heading toward the North Fork of the Teton Canyon for some backcountry skiing and a winter assault of Mt. Wright. It was the Christmas season and the saloon in Choteau, full of warmth and holiday revelers, was a most attractive preliminary stop. The cheer of the folks dancing to western music made it difficult to leave. Still, we were excited to meet winter head on in the epitome of wilderness, in a region that has given me some of my greatest wildland adventures: the Bob Marshall country.

West of Augusta, Choteau, Bynum and Dupuyer, the sprawling, open Montana prairie is abruptly terminated by the towering walls of the Rocky Mountain Front. For 110 miles, this craggy limestone formation serves as the eastern rampart of the Bob Marshall country. Mountain ranges of this extensive territory have a distinct northwest-southwest axis and are separated by long river valleys, some carved by glaciers. From Ear Mountain, a prominent Front Range peak, it is 60 miles as the eagle flies to the slopes of the equally impressive Swan Range, the Bob's western flank.

Glacier National Park and Marias Pass form the northern border, and the valley of the Blackfoot River is the southern terminus of the Bob Marshall eco-system. Its longest axis, from West Glacier south to Rogers Pass, is 140 miles. The area may be circled by highway, a 380-mile journey, but not a single road crosses it.

This is a land of incredible diversity, a scaled down version of what the western American wilderness once was. Windswept prairie ridges, deep canyons, towering cliffs, dense forests, wild rivers, lush meadows and a diverse wildlife population — all are part of this, the crown jewel of the nation's wilderness system.

With the Continental Divide as its backbone, the Bob Marshall country is considerable in size, grandeur and legend. Comprised of the contiguous 1.5 million-acre Bob Marshall, Great Bear and Scapegoat wilderness areas and almost one million acres of surrounding wildlands, the Bob is home to almost every big game species found in North America, including the endangered grizzly bear. Bald and golden eagles soar from its precipitous canyon walls and timber wolves still roam here.

Two of Montana's blue ribbon trout streams, the South Fork and Middle Fork of the Flathead River, are born from its interior high country. The South Fork gets its start on the southern boundary of the wilderness as the Danaher River, and the Middle Fork commences as a trickle via Strawberry Creek at Badger Pass along the Continental Divide.

Other major streams and rivers emanate from the Divide country. They are the Sun River, draining the area on the east side of the Continental Divide; the South Fork of the Two Medicine River, flowing north toward Glacier National Park; Birch Creek, flowing east from the Divide to the prairie; Badger Creek, rising from peaks of the Front Range and surging eastward; and the Dearborn River, making its headwaters along the east wall of Scapegoat Mountain and rushing southeast to the Missouri River.

This realm is steeped in history acted out by Indians and early-day mountain men. Its alpine passes and river valleys served as passageways for western tribes trekking to the east in search of buffalo on the prairie lands beyond the mountain wall. Lewis and Clark Pass on the southern end and Gateway Pass, the headwaters area for the South Fork of Birch Creek, were favored routes. The Blackfeet Nation controlled lands that border the peaks on the east; to protect their hunting grounds, warriors were sent into the mountains to ambush those heading toward the plains.

At the confluence of the North Fork and South Fork of the Sun, to the west of Gibson Lake, Indians frequented the Medicine Springs. Pictographs are evident in this area, and atop Half Dome Crag, west of Heart Butte, Native Americans received visions from the Great Spirit. Travois tracks on the Great North Trail, used by prehistoric man and by Indian tribes in recent history, are still discernable along the Rocky Mountain Front.

The Rocky Mountain Front, with its celebrated relief and towering limestone walls rising upward of 1,000 feet or more from the prairie, is the eastern-most range. Steamboat and Ear mountains, as well as Castle and Sawtooth reefs, are prominent for 50 miles or more to travelers pointing west across the high plains of northern Montana. It was the abrupt rise of this massif that gave the name *land of the shining mountains* to Montana. In the summer of 1805, while moving against the current of the Missouri toward the Rockies, Meriwether Lewis in his journal noted the *"shining Mountains"* to the west, explaining that the sun glancing off of the snow gave the mountains a *"glittering appearance."*

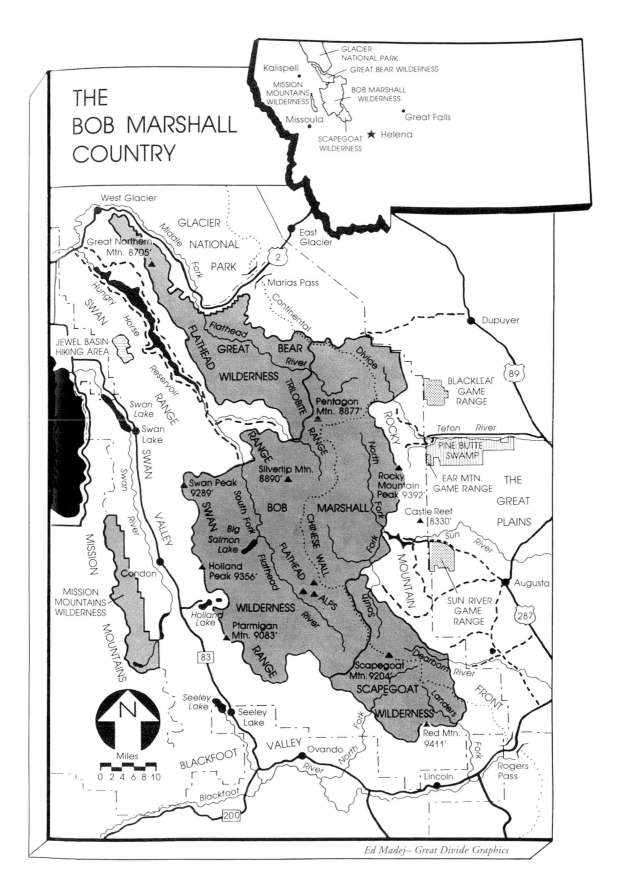

THE BOB MARSHALL COUNTRY

GLACIER NATIONAL PARK
GREAT BEAR WILDERNESS
BOB MARSHALL WILDERNESS

Kalispell
MISSION MOUNTAINS WILDERNESS
Missoula
Great Falls
SCAPEGOAT WILDERNESS
★ Helena

West Glacier
GLACIER NATIONAL PARK
Great Northern Mtn. 8705'
Middle Fork
East Glacier
2
Marias Pass
Continental
Dupuyer
Hungry Horse
SWAN
Flathead
GREAT BEAR WILDERNESS
River
Divide
89
Reservoir
TRILOBITE RANGE
BLACKLEAF GAME RANGE
JEWEL BASIN HIKING AREA
Pentagon Mtn. 8877'
Teton River
Swan Lake
RANGE
North
PINE BUTTE SWAMP
Swan Lake
Silvertip Mtn. 8890'
Rocky Mountain Peak 9392'
EAR MTN. GAME RANGE
THE
RANGE
Swan Peak 9289'
BOB MARSHALL
ROCKY
GREAT
SWAN
South Fork
Castle Reef 8330'
PLAINS
Big Salmon Lake
Fork
CHINESE WALL
Sun River
MISSION
River
SWAN
FLATHEAD
Flathead
MOUNTAIN
Augusta
Condon
Holland Peak 9356'
ALPS
SUN RIVER GAME RANGE
287
MISSION MOUNTAINS WILDERNESS
VALLEY
WILDERNESS
River
Smith
Holland Lake
Ptarmigan Mtn. 9083'
83
Dearborn River
FRONT
MOUNTAINS
RANGE
Scapegoat Mtn. 9204'
Landers
Seeley Lake
SCAPEGOAT
N
Seeley Lake
WILDERNESS
Red Mtn. 9411'
Fork
Miles
0 2 4 6 8 10
BLACKFOOT
VALLEY
Ovando
North
Lincoln
Rogers Pass
River
Fork
Blackfoot
200

Ed Madej– Great Divide Graphics

11

From the top of Mt. Wright. Photo taken July 9, 1945. U.S. FOREST SERVICE PHOTO

The Front stands out as the best known of the ranges, not only because of its geographic location, but also because of controversy and popularity. Energy companies, who have been petitioning the U.S. Forest Service and the Bureau of Land Management for rights to explore for oil and gas here, continue to run into tremendous public opposition. People, some who may never see the backcountry of the Bob Marshall or the Front, rally to help in the good fight. Why? To them, as well as to those who have visited it, the Bob Marshall country and the Rocky Mountain Front are the "*type specimen*," the artist's first wax. They are the essence of wild country, and these folks are happy to know such places exist.

The valleys of the Two Medicine, Sun and Dearborn rivers separate the Rocky Mountain Front from the Continental Divide Range. The impressive features of this watershed chain are the incredible 13-mile-long Chinese Wall and the Scapegoat Mountain complex.

Spotted Bear, the Middle Fork of the Flathead, the White and several other rivers come between the Divide and a central massif of mountains. The Flathead Range to the east of Hungry Horse Lake is the northern segment. Great Northern Mountain is the most visible summit in the area. Prominent points farther south are Silvertip and Pagoda mountains and the Flathead Alps — a cluster of peaks just south of the Chinese Wall including Junction Mountain and Pearl Basin country.

The big valley formed by the South Fork of the Flathead and Danaher rivers separates these central uplifts from the Bob's western-most mountains, the Swan Range. The Swan Peaks, and those adjoining it to the south and east, including those near the town of Lincoln and the Monture Creek country, represent the largest of the mountain masses of the Bob Marshall country.

Compared to other Montana mountains, the summits of the Bob Marshall are vertically challenged — none top 10,000 feet. Red Mountain, at 9,411 feet, is the highest. However, due to their imposing relief, these peaks appear to soar higher than most. Heavy snow loads, especially in the Swan Range and just south of Glacier Park, have helped maintain a few high cirque glaciers.

These small alpine ice fields, existing on the slopes of Swan Peak, Holland Peak and Great Northern Mountain, are remnants of the big valley glaciers that helped sculpture the wilderness.

The wildlands of the Bob Marshall, Scapegoat and Great Bear are known for their mixture of big meadows and dense forest cover. This pristine country abounds with ponderosa, larch, Douglas fir and lodgepole pine, as well as aspen and cottonwood trees. Purple and blue lupine intermingle with the red and orange shades of Indian paint brush on open slopes; yellow columbine, purple twining clematis, blue harebells, the elusive, mountain orchid the lady slipper, and the wispy fragrant bedstraw are strewn along cool forested trails. The meadows along the east side of the Chinese Wall and Scapegoat Mountain present some of the most stunning displays of bear grass in Montana.

Virtually all the terrain of the wilderness country and surrounding land is under U.S. Forest Service management and is accessible to the public. The sharp rise of the Swan Range and a dearth of canyons limit access on the west, but all other areas are reached easily by roads to or near the wilderness boundary. The Rocky Mountain Front on

Spotted Bear Ranger Station in July 1923. U.S. FOREST SERVICE PHOTO

Scapegoat-Halfmoon Park on left, Green Fork drainage on the right. U.S. FOREST SERVICE PHOTO

the east and the southern area have the most entry points. Horse travel is a popular way to visit the backcountry and many outfitters and guides offer trips for sightseeing, hunting, fishing and floating. Backpacking, snowshoeing and skiing are probably the most intimate ways to explore this big land. An excellent trail system provides routes in all directions. The roads that lead into or near the wilderness boundary provide a great sampling of what is available in the backcountry. Forest Service campgrounds along these routes are for the enjoyment of those not able to, or not desiring to, hike the land beyond.

The Bob may be visited any time of the year, but it is easiest to travel the backcountry in the summer months. Spring, with its melting snows and high run-offs, is perhaps the least desirable time. Peak run-off can occur between early May and mid-June. By mid-June most of the smaller streams can be crossed. The bigger waterways are still running fast and deep until about the second week in July.

The heaviest human use is from early July until early September. Later, and on into November, come the hunters. Travel, especially beyond the trails, without skis or snowshoes, becomes difficult after mid-November, and sometimes sooner.

In recent years, Montana sportsmen have established three Rocky Mountain Front wildlife preserves — the Sun River, Ear Mountain and Blackleaf game ranges — to protect the wildlife population. Other private efforts, such as the Teddy Roosevelt Ranch and the Nature Conservancy of Montana's Pine Butte Swamp Preserve — where the grizzlies continue to roam the prairie as they did when Lewis and Clark came through — add to the public's awareness of this phenomenal landscape. Today, because of all of these entities' concerns, the elk and deer population of the Rocky Mountain Front area is far greater than at the turn of the century, and the big horn sheep herd that makes a living here is one of the largest and most important in the nation.

What follows is an attempt to portray the Bob Marshall country by way of text and photography. We have asked others with a special knowledge of certain subjects to contribute their work. The text and the photographs will be easier to follow with a map for reference. The Bob Marshall, Great Bear and Scapegoat Wilderness Complex Map, available through the USFS and outdoor shops, is the best.

Approximately 1,849 miles of trail extend throughout the Bob Marshall wilderness complex. This total does not include trails outside the boundaries of the three wilderness areas. There are extensive ribbons of those in the nearly one million acres of wildlands contiguous to the designated wilderness. For instance, it is about six miles from the trailhead of the West Fork of the Teton to Teton Pass and the Bob's boundary.

The trail system got its official start in 1903 when the USFS constructed a route extending from Ovando to the Danaher Meadows, a distance of 21 miles.

Although trails and access are discussed, they are not covered in-depth; maps show all this. It is my hope that this book will give you the insight to pick your own routes of travel and to challenge you to find your favorite spots.

Offering a myriad of wilderness experiences, the Bob Marshall country has created for me a priceless collection of memories: standing atop the Chinese Wall with a fresh wind blowing in my face ... a full moon illuminating snow-covered Silvertip Mountain ... storm clouds lifting to unveil the sheer face of the Swan Range ... stars so brilliant they beg you to touch them ... peaceful walks through Big River Meadows ... hundreds of elk grazing on the slopes above the North Fork of the Sun ... skiing untracked deep powder near Circle Creek ... picking wild strawberries along the South Fork of Birch Creek ... fly fishing the wild South Fork of the Flathead ... lightning striking the rocks around me on top of Scapegoat Mountain ... virtually swimming in a sea of bear grass along Halfmoon Creek ... being on the summit of Mount Wright at 40 below zero viewing countless rainbows floating in the ice-crystal-filled air of the valleys below ... gazing in awe at the incredible expanse of wild country stretched out before me from the top of Rocky Mountain Peak ... reveling in an impromptu outdoor banjo concert at the Beartop Lookout Tower ... and hearing a wolf greet the dawn with song at Gates Park.

Representing many things to many people, this untamed territory is a chance to experience wilderness at its best. It is a charmer, a caster of spells, a silver-tongued devil that captures your soul. One visit will convince almost anyone that wilderness is worth having. The Bob Marshall country is indeed a national treasure and thanks to the foresight of early-day conservationists, these magnificent mountains, canyons, rivers and valleys will remain wild and free.

BOB MARSHALL, HIS VISION WAS HIS LEGACY

by Sherry Devlin reprinted with permission from The Missoulian

Bob Marshall is credited with single-handedly adding 5.4 million acres to the nation's wilderness system, and in 1941, two years after his death, 950,000 acres of western Montana wilderness were set aside in his name.

The first snow that September was as unpredictable — and fierce — as ever. In a few short hours, the season catapulted from late summer, across autumn and smack into the frigid middle of January. Flowers and berries disappeared under the snowy blanket. Moss-topped boulders turned to icy blocks. The path muddled. Everything that made the forest warm and colorful had vanished.

Now, as nightfall approached, the young woodsman was soaked and chilled — and lost in a howling snowstorm high on the Lolo Trail, somewhere in Montana or Idaho.

"*I stopped in the soggy twilight to look at the map,*" he later wrote, "*and observed with concern a discrepancy between my imagined position and the compass. With a cold, shrinking feeling in my stomach, I went over in my mind all the instructions, every fork, in the trail, and could not recall a single dubious turn.*"

But young Bob Marshall had come West for a taste of the pioneer life, and a night alone in the howling winter wilderness promised just such an adventure. "*On a snowy September night, a century and a quarter before,*" he remembered, "*Lewis and Clark had been camped here, two years from the nearest settlement, winter closing in, food almost gone, meat unprocurable by the best hunters. . . And I was worrying about a single miserable night.*"

Not only did Marshall survive his first scuffle with nature in the wintry Selway Bitterroot Wilderness, but he eventually weathered an Arctic shipwreck, a grizzly attack, scores of assaults on previously unclimbed peaks and innumerable grueling day hikes of 50 miles or more.

By his sudden death — of a heart attack at the age of 38 — Marshall was himself a legend, a 20th-century Lewis and Clark, the first white man to scale Alaska's central Brooks Range, a best-selling author, a radical bureaucrat and tireless advocate of wilderness preservation.

Marshall is credited with single-handedly adding 5.4 million acres to the nation's wilderness system and 16 natural reserves to Indian lands. He lobbied for preservation of Alaska's freezing winter lands long before other conservationists took up the cry. And in 1935, he was the catalyst around which the Wilderness Society was created.

In 1941, two years after Marshall's death, 950,000 acres of western Montana wilderness were set aside in his memory. Today, the Bob Marshall Wilderness is the acknowledged crown jewel of American wildlands — a fitting tribute to the man who once wrote: "*We can afford to sacrifice any other value for the sake of retaining something of the primitive.*"

Born to a wealthy Manhattan family in 1901, Marshall spent his city-bound boyhood "*dreaming of Lewis and Clark and their glorious exploration into the unbroken wilderness which embraced three-quarters of a continent.*"

"*Occasionally, my reveries ended in terrible depression,*" he later recalled, "*and I would imagine that I had been born a century too late for genuine excitement.*"

Then young Marshall discovered the reddish-brown reports of the "*Topographical Survey of the Adirondack Wilderness,*" tucked away at the bottom of a bookcase in his family's summer retreat on Lower Saranac Lake, N.Y.

"*Immediately, he became enthralled by the accounts of explorations in the mountains which surrounded us,*" wrote his brother George. "*We determined to penetrate those mountains, which previously had been accepted as a scenic backdrop along the skyline across the lake.*"

At first, the brothers were content with walks around Lower Saranac Lake. Then came the fish pond and pathless woods. Then the floating bog. "*Every ridge and hollow and deer runway within the forest where we lived became familiar to Bob and he gave them such names as Found Knife Pass, Squashed Berry Valley and Hidden Heaven Rock.*" George remembered.

On August 15, 1916, the Marshall boys climbed their first Adirondack peak — Ampersand — a 3,365-foot mountain south of their summer home. Six years later, the Marshalls — together with old-time Adirondack guide Herb Clark — had climbed 42 of the region's 46 peaks above 4,000 feet. Eventually they climbed all 46.

Marshall had found his "*genuine excitement.*"

"*The sense of adventure which one gets in the wilderness reaches its perfection in the romance of mountaineering,*" he wrote more than 20 years later. The glory of conquering a summit which has baffled humanity by its ruggedness throughout all the passage of world history up to the present moment affords elation to which nothing could equal.

VOL. XXIII, NO. 24   WASHINGTON, D. C.   NOVEMBER 27, 1939

ROBERT MARSHALL, FORESTER — CRUSADER

No man ever rode the crest of the wave of life with higher purpose or more joyousness than Bob Marshall. In electing his way of life, Bob chose mainly those activities which would help to make life better for those who need a hand or would preserve the quality of naturalness of some of our wild land. His ability to walk sixty miles a day in any man's country, and to finish with a spring in his step, typified the zest with which he tackled everything. He was as interested in a whimsical "study" of the dinner-table conversation of lumberjacks as in the I. Q. tests he made on Eskimos and his studies of Arctic vegetation. He was as passionately devoted to the development of organization camps for outings for the underprivileged children as to the preservation of wildernesses where those of special vigor and love of solitude might find adventure. And never a thought of personal prestige in any of his projects or his gifts to good causes.

Death came with shocking suddenness. Bob left Washington Friday night, November 10, on the Pullman for New York for a week-end family gathering. He was apparently in good health, and was looking forward eagerly to the family reunion. His death was discovered on the arrival of the train in New York, and was evidently due to coronary thrombosis.

Men like Marshall can ill be spared. He was a force for many good movements. He had the mental and physical vigor to drive ahead and to inspire and arouse enthusiasm in others. His joyousness and his lively sense of humor were contagious. His capacity for friendship had no bounds. He was "Bob" to hosts — from Justices of the Supreme Court to his beloved friends of the Arctic. Surely no man ever had more friends to mourn him.

But Bob would not want to be mourned. His going was shockingly premature, but he was not afraid to go. He came close to death in Alaska last summer. If there is a Valhalla for the spirits of men, may Bob's spirit find there one of his beloved wilderness areas — something to bring forth that expression we often heard him use, "Gee, this is swell!".

F. A. SILCOX.

Chief.

Long before graduating from New York City's Ethical Culture High School, Marshall had decided on a career in forestry and conservation. *"I didn't have the remotest idea what forestry was,"* he once stated, *"but I had vague notions of thrilling adventures with bad men, of lassoing infuriated grizzlies and of riding down unknown canyons in Alaska."*

Then, too, there was the example set by his father. An internationally known constitutional lawyer and Jewish community leader, Louis Marshall led the fight in 1914 to retain New York's *"forever wild"* guarantee for Adirondack State Park. He was a pioneer in bird protection reform and spoke harshly against the country's *"hasty dismantling of her natural heritage."*

The lesson wasn't lost on his son. In 1920, after a year at Columbia University, Bob Marshall enrolled at New York State College of Forestry — where his father was a trustee.

But young Marshall still yearned for adventure. Immediately after graduation in 1924, he headed for a summer of mountain climbing and research at the Wind River Forest Experiment Station, near the Columbia River, in southwestern Washington.

In the spring of 1925, Marshall received his master's degree in forestry from Harvard and again headed West — this time to the Northern Rocky Mountain Forest and Range Experiment Station in Missoula. There he stayed for three years working his way from Junior forester to assistant silviculturist.

It was in Missoula that the Marshall legend began.

"A real greyhound" in the words of one Forest Service colleague, junior forester Marshall spent nearly all his free time in the backwoods of Montana and Idaho.

It was there, one September afternoon, that he wandered off the course in a blinding snowstorm. And there, too, that he came upon a pair of grizzly cubs one sunny summer morning.

"I stood watching their unconcerned antics with great interest," Marshall wrote in his Journal, *"until all at once I heard a crashing noise behind. Wheeling around I saw a colossal grizzly, not 30 feet away, charging straight at me."*

"'There's not to reason why, there's but to climb or die,' so I started on the run for a white bark pine which seemed to offer the closest haven. Up I went, faster than my unaerial anatomy had ever progressed toward heaven. Up I went for about 10 feet, when in my haste I stepped too clumsily on a dead branch. It snapped and I flopped."

Marshall survived the grizzly sow's charge by playing dead. But he eventually contributed to his premature death by subjecting an already-frail heart to tortuous hikes in the Bitterroots, Flatheads, Missions, Cascades and Selkirks. Rarely was a day hike less than 40 miles; most totaled 50 or more.

"Up in northern Idaho, Bob decided to walk around the head of the East River drainage and back to the Priest River Forest Experiment Station," remembered retired forester Chuck Wellner in a recent interview. *"When he got back to Priest River and discovered he had traveled only 45 miles, he walked another five miles down the road so he could log a full 50."*

Ralph Space, retired supervisor of Idaho's Clearwater National Forest, told of a 5O-miler that Marshall made from Moose Creek Ranger Station in the Nez Perce Forest to the Bitterroot Valley near Hamilton.

"My fellas told me that when Marshall came in over the divide, he was so exhausted he would stumble, fall, lay there for a while and then hike some more," Space said. *"He kept a record of any time he hiked over 50 miles. He really drove himself to the extremes."*

By the time he was 36 — two years before his death — Marshall had logged more than 200 wilderness hikes of 30 miles in a day, 51 hikes of more than 40 miles and several of up to 70 miles.

"Toting a 50-pound pack over an abominable trail, snowshoeing across a blizzard swept plateau or scaling some jagged pinnacle which juts far above timber," Marshall maintained, *"all develop a body distinguished by a soundness, stamina and elan unknown amid normal surroundings."*

And Marshall did indeed love the wilderness. *"It is the perfect aesthetic experience,"* he told Nature magazine readers in 1937. *"It is vast panoramas, full of height and depth and flowing color on a scale so overwhelming as to wipe out the ordinary meaning of dimensions. It is the song of the hermitt thrush at twilight. It is the unique odor of balsams and of freshly turned humus. It is the feel of spruce needles underfoot."*

A personable man, *"filled with humor,"* Marshall had little trouble finding wilderness converts among his friends. *"He loved the feeling of wilderness — the animals, forests and waters,"* said ecologist-writer Siguard Olson in a telephone interview from his Ely, Minn., home.

"When Bob shared his feelings and experiences, whether in his writing or speaking, he had tremendous impact," Olson said. *"If he had lived even a normal life span, the history of our country and its wild places would have been a different story."*

But Marshall probably wasn't cut out to be a *"true scientist,"* said retired forester Wellner, who had a long career as assistant director of the Intermountain Forest and Range Experiment Station in Ogden, Utah.

"His real love was the wilderness, not the office or research lab," Wellner said. *"When I took over Bob's old records in Missoula, there were hundreds of notes scribbled on little scraps of paper. He just wasn't too keen on details."*

Marshall also left behind hundreds of *"tall but true"* tales when he journeyed back East in 1928 to study for a doctorate at Johns Hopkins University.

"Like the one about the time we was going to a dance in Missoula," Willner said. *"Harry Gisborne (the fire research pioneer) was a great friend of Bob's. Harry's wife, Alice, noticed that Bob had a hole in his sock right above the heel. So Bob got some black ink, painted his heel and went on to the dance."*

Seasoned by his years in the West, and by the first of four treks to far northern Alaska, Marshall wrote his most important wilderness thesis while at Johns Hopkins. Marshall called it *"The Problem of the Wilderness."* His admirers called it *"The Magna Carta of the Wilderness Movement."*

In the Scientific Monthly report, Marshall warned that the *"shrunken remnants of an undefiled continent are being despoiled."* Valleys that once knew *"only footsteps of wild animals."* now know the terrors of modern highways, he said. Gone is the ground cover of fresh sorrel and twinflower. Here to stay is *"asphalt spotted with chewing gum, coal dust and gasoline."*

"Within the next few years the fate of the wilderness must be decided," he said. *"This is a problem to be settled by deliberate rationality and not by personal prejudice."* What followed was a step-by-step rationale for the preservation of wild country.

Anticipating protests by timber companies, Marshall explained that *"what small financial loss ultimately results from the establishment of wilderness areas must be accepted as a fair price to pay for their unassessable preciousness."*

The doctrine of *"the greatest good to the greatest number"* does not apply to every acre on earth, Marshall said. *"If it did,"* he wrote later, *"we would be forced to change our metropolitan art galleries into metropolitan bowling alleys. The Library of Congress would become a national hot dog stand, and the new Supreme Court building would be converted into a gigantic garage where it could house a thousand people's autos instead of Nine Gentlemen of the Law."*

What was needed, then, Marshall concluded, was *"the organization of spirited people who will fight for the freedom of the wilderness."* Without their help, *"there will be countless souls born to live in strangulation,"* he said, *"countless human beings who will be crushed under the artificial edifice raised by man."*

The seeds of the wilderness movement thus planted and a doctorate in hand, Marshall fulfilled his lifelong dream early in 1931 — and left for a 13-month sojourn to the basin of the Koyukuk River in Alaska.

There he found Wiseman, a self-sustaining Arctic hunting and mining village of 77 whites, 44 Eskimos and six Indians spread over a land as large as Massachusetts and New Jersey combined.

Content as he never would be in Washington. D.C., Marshall mapped the Koyukuk drainage and much of the central Brooks Range. He scaled a long line of previously unclimbed peaks, named hundreds of geographic features (like Frigid Crags, Midnight Mountain and Blarney Creek) and relished in *"the most glorious year of my life."*

His return to the east in 1932 brought Marshall's greatest literary success, the publication of *"Arctic Village"* Forum magazine called it *"the personal biography of a wilderness settlement."* Others heralded it as a *"valuable sociological document fit to join the works of Margaret Mead."*

But for Marshall, *"Arctic Village"* was a testimonial to all that is right about wilderness and life in the wilderness. *"The Inhabitants of Koyukuk,"* he wrote, *"would rather eat beans with liberty, bum candles with independence and mush dogs with adventure than to brave the luxury and the restrictions of the outside world. A person misses many things by living in the isolation of Koyukuk, but he gains a life filled with an amount of freedom, tolerance, beauty and contentment few human beings are ever fortunate enough to achieve."*

His return from Alaska also brought Marshall's first major report for the Forest Service — *"The Forest for Recreation and a Program for Forest Recreation."* part of the National Plan for American Forestry submitted to Congress in 1933.

Marshall was now more convinced than ever that America's wild lands were in jeopardy. *"The universe of the wilderness, all over the United States, is vanishing with appalling rapidity,"* he wrote. *"It is melting away like the last snow bank on some south-facing mountainside during a hot afternoon in June."*

The solution, he said, was the protection of 45 million acres — 9 percent of the nation's commercial timberland. Of that amount, 3 million acres would be *"superlative scenic areas"* like Yellowstone or Yosemite and 9.5 million acres would be *"primeval areas or tracts of virgin timber in which human activities have never upset the normal processes of nature."*

A third category — wilderness areas — required set-asides of at least 10 million acres in Marshall's plan. *"And by wilderness,"* he said, *"I mean regions sufficiently spacious that a person may spend at least a week or two of travel in them without crossing his own tracks."*

The remaining 12.5 million acres, then, would be divided between roadside scenic areas, campsites, forest residence areas and non-wilderness outing areas. And rather than ruin commercial timber interests, Marshall said, his plan would actually increase the value of their land.

The trick, he claimed, was proper forest management — which in Marshall's book meant nationalization of timberlands. *"Public ownership is the only basis from which we can hope to protect the incalculable values of forest for wood resources, for soil and water conservation and for recreations,"* he wrote in The People's Forests.

"The time has come," Marshall said, *"when we must discard the unsocial view that our woods are the lumberman's and substitute the broader ideal that every acre of woodland in the country is rightly a part of the people's forests."*

Retired Clearwater Forest Supervisor Space spent many an hour debating the nationalization of timberland with Marshall. *"We talked quite a bit about Bob's high regard for communistic funs of government,"* Space said. *"He believed that goods should be produced for service, not profit."*

And while socialist and communist theories were popular during the depths of the Great Depression, it was *"unusual to hear a millionaire advocate that kind of system,"* Space said.

Marshall, who inherited a fortune from his father, eventually left $750,000 to a foundation *"for the promotion and advancement of an economic system in the United States based on the theory of production for use and not for profit."* Marshall's will entrusted another $400,000 to his friends in the Wilderness Society with the stipulation that it would be used to *"increase the knowledge of the citizens of the United States as to the importance and necessity maintaining wilderness conditions in outdoor America for future generations."*

"He was a wealthy guy, all right," remembered Clyde Fickes, *"He was a protégé of Mrs. Franklin Delano Roosevelt and both of them had all kinds of money. If he wanted to fly to New Guinea, he didn't have to worry about it."*

Still, Marshall preferred a simple life and in 1933 accepted the post of Forestry Director for the U.S. Office of Indian Affairs. There he pushed his wilderness work to the forefront lobbying the Interior Department for more roadless areas, setting aside wilderness areas on Indian reservations and organizing the Wilderness Society.

He wasn't without his detractors, however. Once, confronted by a particularly reactionary congressman, Marshall fired off this response: *"Because I've been out in the woods and up in the Arctic a good part of the past five years, it may be that the Bill of Rights was repealed without my hearing about it."*

[In] 1937 when Marshall was named Chief of the Forest Service Division of Recreation and Lands, he finally was in the right place at the right time to turn his wilderness advocacy into action.

Every roadless area of more than 100,000 acres should be protected as *"primitive land,"* Marshall said. And for every proposed highway, irrigation project or lumbering job, there should be a comparison of values: *"Do the increased benefits of this extension of civilization really compensate for the loss of wilderness values?"*

Taking to the road with a fervor often unknown in bureaucratic circles, Marshall set out to *"inspect"* the wilderness he wanted to protect. In August 1937, the trek was to northern Minnesota for a weeklong canoe trip with ecologist-author Olson.

"Bob was full of enthusiasm for the canoe country," Olson said. *"We paddled all through what is now the Boundary Waters Canoe Area and Canada's Quetico Provincial Park. He told me that something inside of him needed to get out in the wilderness — so that's what he did."*

In 1938, the call went out to Mississippi where now retired forester Roswell Leavitt *"left him off along the road so he could hike 10 miles or so through the second growth southern pines."* Another week it was New Mexico and an impromptu hike through desert brush and scrub pine.

"It was a good way of life for Bob," his brother George later wrote. *"He enjoyed people just as much as the wilderness and needed both. He had a splendid sense of humor, great gusto and infectious enthusiasm."*

The summers of 1938 and 1939 also found Marshall back among the people of Koyukuk and central Brooks Range. On his final journey, Marshall was shipwrecked in icy Arctic waters. *"What an awfully easy way to die,"* he wrote. *"I kept saying to myself: 'Gosh, I wish I had time to think over all the swell experiences of my 37 years before dying — to have the fun of recalling them just once more before I go.'"*

As fate would have it, Marshall had only a few months to live when he returned to Washington. D.C., after his final Alaska adventure. But in that time, he celebrated one of his greatest successes — adoption by the Forest Service of the *"U"* regulations, which prohibited logging in wilderness areas.

In November 1939, when Marshall died in his sleep while on a train to New York, his colleagues and friends

Bob Marshall. WILDERNESS SOCIETY PHOTO

were stunned. "*If there is a Valhalla for the spirits of men, may Bob's spirit find there one of his beloved wilderness areas,*" wrote Forest Service Chief F.A. Silcox.

"*He was the one guy who could always pull you out of the squirrel cage and make you feel again the excitement, importance and opportunity in what you were trying to do,*" added a New Republic editorial.

"*With his passing the cause of wilderness preservation lost one of its greatest champions,*" said ecologist Olson. "*He would not be surprised to see that the battle for wilderness preservation is still raging. But he would be disheartened to see that even an area named in his memory is under attack.*"

The Bob Marshall Wilderness, after years of relative quiet, has erupted recently into a major battleground between wilderness advocates and oil and gas companies. Industry wants the Bob Marshall opened to exploration and development; conservationists want it protected. The battle is currently mired in the courts and halls of Congress.

But Marshall knew the fight for wilderness would not be an easy one and, a year before his death, he penned what many believe to be his most fitting eulogy:

"*We're all young enough that we'll probably meet many defeats in the next 50 years. It's even conceivable that when we die we still will not have won the fight. But win or lose, it will be grand fun fighting and knowing that whatever we do in the right direction will help eventual victory.*"

Sherry Devlin worked as the Missoula. Montana's Missoulian's natural resources and environment reporter.

Top: Fairview Creek taken in 1925.   U.S. FOREST SERVICE PHOTO
Bottom: The North Fork of the Sun River country in the area of Two Shacks Flat in March of 1917.   U.S. FOREST SERVICE PHOTO

CREATION OF THE BOB MARSHALL WILDERNESS
by Rick and Susie Graetz

In 1897, President Grover Cleveland established the Lewis and Clark Forest Reserve under the provisions of the Forest Reserve Act. At that time the Reserves were administered by the Department of the Interior. In 1905, the Forest Service was created along with the Department of Agriculture and in 1907, the Forest Reserves became known as National Forests. Until 1910, Glacier National Park was part of the Lewis and Clark National Forest Reserve, then the area was given national-park status.

On August 16, 1940, Secretary of Agriculture Henry A. Wallace designated the 950,000-acre Bob Marshall Wilderness, which was formed by combining three previously designated National Forest Primitive Areas — the South Fork, established in 1931; the Sun River, established in 1934; and Pentagon, established in 1933.

The boundaries of the original primitive areas seem to have been determined by hydrological divides. The South Fork of the Flathead, the Sun River and the Middle Fork of the Flathead are the three major drainages in the area. The Pentagon Primitive Area was often called the Big River Primitive Area, a name commonly given to the Middle Fork of the Flathead River.

The Great Falls Tribune, on February 24, 1934, reported the "*Plan to create a primitive area on Upper Sun River approved by FA Silcox. Boundaries-Black Reef west of Allan Ranch, across North Fork Sun River-up Sheep Reef to divide between the Teton River and North Fork of Sun: thence northwest along Continental Divide to head of Basin Creek and west between West Fork River and South Fork Sun River, thence along Black Reef to North Fork Sun River,*" The Allan ranch referred to in this article is today the Klick ranch at the confluence of the North and South Forks of the Sun.

The following is a copy of the original Forest Service document recommending the designation of the Bob Marshall Wilderness Area.

BOB MARSHALL WILDERNESS AREA

A great "back country" mountain and mountain-valley territory lying astride the Continental Divide in the Flathead and Lewis and Clark National Forests in western Montana, as more definitely shown on attached map.

The area includes and is bounded coincidentally with the limits of "primitive areas" of several years standing established under Regulation L-20:

> South Fork - designated May 20, 1931.
> Pentagon - designated October 18, 1933, enlarged July 5, 1939.
> Sun River - designated February 23, 1934.

These will continue to be called the South Fork Unit, Pentagon Unit and Sun River Unit of the Bob Marshall Wilderness Area, with minor changes of boundary to insure that the titles are truly significant.

Establishment of a wilderness area composed of these three primitive area units will involve no present change in requirements, since the particular restrictions added, at the time of their designation, to the restrictions under Regulation L-20, bring the provisions well within the requirements of Regulation U-1. Advertisement and 90 days' notice will not be necessary. The condition imposed, as no. 7 in the designation of February 23, 1934, for the Sun River Unit, making the designation subject to the existing First Form Reclamation Withdrawal, will, of course, continue.

The aggregate acreage will approximate 950,000 - area largely unsurveyed, the figure cannot be more precise. Of this aggregate, approximately 8% in odd-numbered sections in the extreme southwest part is alienated.

There is no demand for timber. Range use by domestic stock is limited to saddle and pack animals. The tract is of highest importance for watershed protection, especially on the Atlantic side of the Divide.

The country has great and outstanding natural and primitive allure, which has attracted constantly increasing numbers of visitors even before its primitive area designation. Inspiring are the spectacular scenery and indisturbed naturalness of the less rugged main stream valleys. Despite substantial use in some spots, wild life and good fishing continue abundant everywhere.

The Sun River and South Fork Units are already quite well known nationally as well as locally by all interested in wilderness areas. Local public sentiment has staunchly supported establishment of the primitive areas, and no questions are expected in regard to the change here recommended.

This area was one of the first in which "Bob" Marshall made his explorations and hikes in this region. He was largely instrumental in its continuance in primitive condition. It is one of outstanding and well known wilderness areas that was among the earliest designated. It conforms fully to the ideal conception of a wilderness area. A worthy monument, indeed, does it make to his memory.

Appropriate favorable action is strongly recommended to redesignate the existing primitive areas into one wilderness area as indicated.

August 10, 1940	_Evan Kelley_
Date	Regional Forester

Approved:

August 15, 1940	_Earle H Clapp_
Date	Acting Chief, Forest Service

Approved:

August 16, 1940.	_H A Wallace_
Date	Secretary of Agriculture

Scapegoat and Great Bear

The Scapegoat Wilderness Area was designated by Congress in 1972 and the Great Bear Wilderness in 1978 along with additions to the Bob Marshall Wilderness. These two areas contiguous to the Bob Marshall Wilderness, along with unroaded wildlands surrounding the designated places comprise what we call Bob Marshall country.

GEOLOGY OF THE BOB
by Dave Alt

In one form and another, the overthrust belt winds a varied, and more or less disconnected, course from the arctic end of the Canadian Rockies to Central America. But the province is not nearly as simple as a long, curving line on a map might suggest. Geologists who try to trace the overthrust belt find that its different segments consist of quite different rock formations; and it is difficult to find several geologists who can easily agree on exactly how one segment connects with the next.

However, all portions of the overthrust belt do resemble each other in being composed of rock formations that slid generally eastward, perhaps 50 miles or more, during formation of the Rocky Mountains. That happened slowly, probably during a period of several million years and it did not happen at the same time in all parts of the overthrust belt. In round numbers, we can say that it happened about 70 million years ago, give or take 10 million or so years. That was about the time that the dinosaurs reached the peak of their development, and then abruptly vanished — there is no reason to suppose that the two events were in anyway related.

Now, the displaced rocks of the overthrust belt exist in complexly jumbled structures in which older formations tend to lie on top of younger ones, exactly the reverse of their normal order. That arrangement formed through generally eastward sliding during development of the Rocky Mountains unites the various segments of the overthrust belt in a loosely continuous geologic province. Let us look more closely at one segment of that province, the northern Montana portion of the overthrust belt.

Considered from a geologic point of view, that portion of the overthrust belt is really a southern extension of the Canadian Rockies. Rocks do not respect political boundaries. The northern Montana portion of the overthrust belt consists of the mountains of Glacier Park, and the Sawtooth Range, which extends from Glacier Park almost to Helena and includes the Bob Marshall and Scapegoat Wilderness areas. All those mountains share the same general geologic history, which begins more than a billion years ago with deposition of the oldest sedimentary formations.

A billion or so years ago, during that remote period geologists call the Precambrian Era, the western margin of our continent was about where the western border of Idaho is day. There were no animals yet, and the highest forms of life were primitive blue-green algae similar to some of those that still form scummy growths in quiet pools of water. Thick sequences of layered sediments destined to become formations of mudstone, sandstone, and limestone were accumulating some in shallow water, others on more or less dry land. Those rocks now form a large and conspicuous part of the northern Montana overthrust belt, virtually all of Glacier Park, and most of the western part of the Sawtooth Range. No one knows how thick the section of Precambrian sedimentary rocks is, but it amounts to some tens of thousands of feet — an enormously thick pile.

Anyone, geologist or not, can rather easily learn to recognize those Precambrian sedimentary rocks. They consist mostly of colorful red and green mudstones, limestones in many shades of gray, and sandstones in a wide spectrum of colors ranging from white through yellow to red. Streams round fragments of those rocks in pebbles that make brightly colorful deposits of gravel, beautiful beds for sparkling mountain streams. People who look closely at individual pebbles, or at the bedrock outcrops from which they came find an abundance of exquisitely preserved sedimentary structures.

Paper-thin sedimentary layers make patterns of fine stripes in many pebbles. The same layers appear in many bedrock outcrops along with perfectly recognizable sand ripples, layers of sun-cracked mud, raindrop imprints, and many other structures. They tell us something about the world of a billion years ago: that waves and running water ruffled soft sand or mud in ripples then just as they do now and that the sun sometimes baked drying mud in intricate patterns of cracks just like those we see in roadside puddles day. Sometimes a passing shower left those mud surfaces imprinted with little dents recording a sprinkle of raindrops. How could such delicate features survive so long?

Many younger sedimentary rocks contain similar structures, but rarely so perfectly preserved, or in such spectacular abundance. The difference seems to lie in the absence of animals from the Precambrian scene. Nothing rooted around in those layers of soft mud and sand as they accumulated so the original sedimentary features remained undisturbed as they were burled and the soft sediments eventually hardened in solid rock.

It is possible to find abundant fossil remains pf blue-green algae in many of the Precambrian sedimentary rocks. They appear in a variety of forms, most commonly as inconspicuous and paper-thin laminations in the rock.

New life comes up after the fire in Teton Pass on the Continental Divide.   RICK AND SUSIES GRAETZ

Top: From the Chinese Wall Trail looking down Rock Creek. RICK AND SUSIE GRAETZ
Bottom: Red Butte and the Chinese Wall. RICK AND SUSIE GRAETZ

Chinese Wall from Moose Creek area.   CARR CLIFTON

Top: The Wrong Creek Guard Station and Wapiti Ridge. RICK AND SUSIE GRAETZ
Bottom: On the North Fork of the Sun Trail through remnants of the 1988 Gates Park fire. RICK AND SUSIE GRAETZ

Top: The North Fork of the Sun River near Moose Creek.   RICK AND SUSIE GRAETZ
Bottom: The Chinese Wall from near Larch Hill Pass.   RICK AND SUSIE GRAETZ

29

Three generations of the Grimes family – l to r, Kevin, Brian and Pat in Teton Pass. RICK AND SUSIES GRAETZ

30

Top: The South Fork of the Sun River. RICK AND SUSIE GRAETZ
Bottom: 9,200-foot Scapegoat Mountain in winter. RICK AND SUSIE GRAETZ

Top: 9,411-foot Red Mountain in the Scapegoat is the highest peak in the Bob Marshall complex. RICK AND SUSIE GRAETZ
Bottom: Dave and Sandi Ashley on Castle Reef looking into Hannan Gulch. RICK AND SUSIE GRAETZ

Beargrass and Scapegoat Mountain.   RICK AND SUSIES GRAETZ

Top: Beargrass in the Great Bear Wilderness. RICK AND SUSIE GRAETZ
Center: From the north slopes of Rocky Mountain Peak looking toward Headquarters Pass and Old Baldy. RICK AND SUSIE GRAETZ
Bottom: Camping below 9,393-foot Rocky Mountain Peak, the highest summit in the Rocky Mountain Front and Bob Marshall proper. RICK AND SUSIE GRAETZ

Lake Levalle and the North Wall.   BOB COONEY

Top: From below Cliff Mountain looking north along the Chinese Wall.   RICK AND SUSIE GRAETZ
Bottom: Mike Munoz and Kraig Lange lead a pack string along the Chinese Wall.   RICK AND SUSIE GRAETZ

Top: A trail crew working on the Chinese Wall Trail. RICK AND SUSIE GRAETZ
Bottom: Beargrass below the Trilobite Range. RICK AND SUSIE GRAETZ

Top: From Prairie Reef looking west toward the Chinese Wall. RICK AND SUSIE GRAETZ
Bottom: Todd Graetz feasts on wild huckleberries in the Great Bear Wilderness.
RICK AND SUSIE GRAETZ

Top: Horses in Gates Park. RICK AND SUSIE GRAETZ
Bottom: North Fork Sun from Arsenic Peak before 1988 fires. RICK AND SUSIE GRAETZ

Looking west toward Pentagon Mountain.   RICK AND SUSIES GRAETZ

Those were simply scummy growths of algae that covered the mud surface and were then buried beneath another accumulation of mud. Here and there, in places where growing conditions were most favorable, the algae developed structures called stromatolites, which look at first glance as though they might be fossil cabbages, although stromatolites and cabbages are related only in that both are plants. Stromatolites may be as small as brussel sprouts, or as large as washtubs, and in many places they form massive reefs. The fossil blue-green algae deserve a certain degree of respect from all of us because they were the first green plants. They started the long process of transforming the earth's early atmosphere in a breathable composition. That made it possible for animals to appear on our planet; and that event ended the Precambrian Era.

The first animals appeared, abruptly and in some considerable variety, about 570 million years ago. That was the beginning of the Cambrian Period and also of the Paleozoic Era, which includes six more geologic periods. Animals evolve continuously, so the changing fashions of their fossil remains subdivide the time since they appeared in a series of geologic periods.

The last of the Precambrian sedimentary rocks seems to have formed sometime before the first animals appeared, perhaps as much as few hundred million years before. Sometime around the middle of Cambrian Time, about 550 million years ago, our region sank slightly below sea level. Cambrian sedimentary rocks, some of them full of animal fossils, accumulated to a total thickness between 1,000 and 2,000 feet. That is only a small fraction of the amount of Precambrian sedimentary rock. Nevertheless, the Cambrian rocks are conspicuous in some parts of the Sawtooth Range because they include massive beds of limestone that make bold cliffs and high ridges. The Chinese Wall, one of the best-known landmarks in the Bob Marshall Wilderness, is a high cliff carved in Cambrian limestone.

The fossils tell us that there is a gap after Cambrian Time and that the next sedimentary rocks began to accumulate during Devonian Time, about 390 million years ago. Layers of sedimentary rock then continued to accumulate, with no extremely long interruptions until the end. The Paleozoic Era, approximately 225 million years ago. Between 5,000 and 6,000 feet, Paleozoic sedimentary rock accumulated after Cambrian Time, and geologists divide it into about a dozen formations. Some of those formations are conspicuous in the landscape of the Sawtooth Range.

It is virtually Impossible to visit the eastern part of the Sawtooth Range without noticing the Madison Limestone. It is about 2,000 feet thick in most areas, and always seems to form grand cliffs and ridges. Including the high ridge that forms the eastern rampart of the range. A close look at outcrops of the Madison Limestone often reveals fossil corals, some of which look almost like honeycombs embedded in the rock. The Jefferson Dolomite is another ridge and cliff-forming body of rock. It is generally dark brown or black, and it stinks when freshly broken. Both the dark color and the foul smell are caused by abundant organic matter trapped in the rock.

The Mesozoic Era began about 225 million years ago as the Paleozoic Era ended, and it lasted until about 65 million years ago. This was the time when the dinosaurs roamed the earth, and their sudden disappearance defines the end of the era. The Mesozoic Era was also a time when more formations of layered sedimentary rocks about 1,500 feet of them, accumulated in our region. None of those rock units makes high ridges: they tend instead to contribute to the landscape by eroding into deep valleys.

Toward the end of Mesozoic Time, when the last of the sedimentary formations were accumulating, volcanoes were erupting in the area between Helena and Butte. Large masses of molten granite magma were rising into the upper part of the earth's crust in that area, and some of it erupted to make a thick pile of volcanic rocks, and to fill the air with clouds of volcanic ash. Much of that volcanic pile has since eroded away to reveal the granite that crystallized beneath it, but enough remains to tell the story. Some of the volcanic ash survives in the late Mesozoic sedimentary rocks in the Sawtooth Range, and along the east side of Glacier Park. We find it in somber greenish sandstones, and in occasional beds of bentonite clay, which is an altered form of volcanic ash.

None of the older sedimentary formations contains volcanic ash. Its appearance in the late Mesozoic rocks signals the beginning of crustal movements that would soon transform our region from a broad plain near sea level to ranges of high mountains. Events in the Northern Rocky Mountains were actually a small part of a much larger pattern that affected much of the earth.

As the Mesozoic Era began, the American continents were joined to Europe and Africa to make an enormous super-continent that included most of the earth's land area. The Atlantic Ocean did not exist then, and the Pacific Ocean was much broader than it is now. Then about 200 million years ago, the super-continent split, pieces began to move apart as the Atlantic Ocean opened between them. That movement yet continues and still causes major geologic activity in many parts of the world. Formation of the Rocky Mountains was one of its earlier consequences.

Something must give if a continent starts moving across the face of the earth. In this case, the floor of the Pacific Ocean buckled and began to slide beneath the western margins of the American continents and then down into the earth's interior. Meanwhile, a new oceanic crust formed in the middle of the Atlantic Ocean as it grew wider. The disappearing floor of the Pacific Ocean was primarily responsible for the creation of the Rocky Mountains and the overthrust belt.

As the sinking oceanic crust reached a depth of about 60 miles, its upper part melted and rose toward the surface. By late Mesozoic time, that was happening on a large scale in the western part of our region, and enormous masses of granite magma were rising in the upper part of the continent in the area that Is now central and northern Idaho and westernmost Montana. Emplacement of those enormous masses of granite, one after the other, over a period of millions of years, bulged the earth's surface up as though there were an enormous blister beneath it. The bubble, that must have been at least several thousand feet high, contributed to formation of the overthrust belt by raising and tilting all those thousands of feet of layered sedimentary rocks that had been accumulating in our region since Precambrian Time.

We think of rocks as rigid and unyielding, because they seem that way in our everyday experience, but ours is a limited and rather unrevealing view. On the scale of the earth's crust and the endless expanses of geologic time, rocks behaved as though they had almost no strength and almost as though they were so much warm gelatin.

Compare the situation of the sedimentary section in the Northern Rockies at the end of Mesozoic Time to that of a thick stack of heavily buttered pancakes on a tilted platter. The result is a perilously unstable situation. One could expect that the stronger rocks, such as limestone or sandstone, behaved in a manner comparable to the pancakes, while the weaker rocks, such as shale, lubricated the stack much like the butter. The entire section of layered sedimentary rocks responded to the tilting by doing about what we would expect of the pancakes — it slid. The layers of rock moved generally eastward because that was the downhill direction and piled up in great slabs to form the complexly jumbled structures that comprise the overthrust belt.

Several pieces of evidence provide clues as to when that all happened. We know that the overthrust belt could not have begun to form much before the end of the Mesozoic Era, because very late Mesozoic sedimentary rocks were involved. On the other hand, the earliest rocks deposited during the succeeding Cenozoic Era are not deformed so movement must have been complete before those sediments accumulated. The time window between those limits reaches from about 75 to about 55 million years ago in round numbers. Other, more subtle clues lead most geologists to believe that overthrust belt deformation must have happened during the earlier part of that period, perhaps about 70 million years ago.

We have no way of knowing exactly how far the slabs of rock in the overthrust belt moved. However, it seems quite likely that many of the rocks in the northern Montana overthrust must have traveled at least 50 miles to reach their present positions. Some may have moved even farther. In other words a large portion of the rocks we see today in the Sawtooth Range and in Glacier Park must have accumulated as sediments in northwestern Montana or possibly even in northern Idaho. The rocks presently at the surface in those regions formed at some considerable depths, so it is perfectly conceivable that they are exposed now because the rocks that formerly covered them moved off and into the overthrust belt.

Neither is it possible to know exactly how long it look, the rocks in the overthrust belt to move into their present positions. But we can be sure that there is no reason to suppose they moved rapidly. Most geologists assume that the rocks moved very slowly, probably during a period of at least several million years. For example, if the rocks moved at the rate of one inch per year, they could travel 50 miles within about three million years. That is what most geologists envision even though they have no solid information on the actual rate of movement.

Visitors to the Rocky Mountain Front notice almost immediately that the landscape is built on a basic framework of high ridges and deep valleys that continue for many miles. This distinctive landscape, vividly expresses the geologic structure of the overthrust belt.

Each long ridge is the outcrop of a resistant layer of rock, each valley the exposure of a layer that wears away easily. The ridges stand high because erosion removed the less resistant rock and carved deep valleys.

A quick look at the landscape shows that the Front Range consists basically of sedimentary rocks tilted gently down to the west. The upturned edges of the layers trend from north to south simply because that direction is at right angles to the way they tilt. Look at the shingles on a roof and see that their edges are at right angles to the direction the roof slopes.

Landscapes consisting of fairly straight and parallel ridges and valleys are fairly common. In most cases, they form where erosion has carved the less resistant layers in a folded or tilted sequence of sedimentary rocks leaving the more resistant layers to stand high as long ridges. However, anyone who learns to recognize even a few of the different rock formations in the Sawtooth Range quickly discovers that the situation there is far more complex than simple folding or tilting. Consider for example the sequence of rock formations along the road through the Sun River Canyon west of Augusta, the place where many visitors first enter the Sawtooth Range (Rocky Mountain Front).

Castle Reef, the high ridge that forms the abrupt eastern front of the Range in the Sun River area is an enormous slab of Madison limestone tilted gently down to the west. Several formations that normally lie on top of the limestone are exposed in the valley west of that ridge, exactly as one would expect. Then things get more complicated. The next ridge west of that valley is another slab of Madison limestone also tilted down to the west. That is absolutely astonishing because the second slab of limestone must lie on top of rock formations younger than itself, the reverse of the normal and proper order. Then the situation repeats itself again with another valley followed by still another high ridge of Madison limestone. The pattern continues beyond the end of the road and westward through the range, except that the rock formations involved become progressively older westward. There is a succession of ridges composed of the Jefferson formation, then the Cambrian limestones and finally various Precambrian formations.

There is only one way to get a big slab of Madison limestone or any other formation on top of rocks younger than itself, and that is by faulting. Those immense slabs of rock must have slid over the younger rocks along a surface that slopes gently down to the west. Geologists call such surface slippage overthrust faults. The Sawtooth Range contains over a dozen large overthrust faults and many numerous lesser ones.

Even now, almost a century after the phenomenon was first recognized, geologists have trouble understanding overthrust faulting. How does a sheet of rock thousands of feet thick that extends over hundreds or even thousands of square miles slide almost horizontally for long distances?

For many years, geologists assumed that something must have pushed those slabs from behind. Unfortunately for that idea, there is nothing behind most of those slabs that could possibly have shoved them. The Swan and Mission valleys lie west of the Sawtooth Range and neither could have given much of a heave-ho. Furthermore, it is easy to show that a force applied from behind would crumple those slabs into folds long before it could overcome the frictional resistance to their movement. The problem is a bit like getting behind a large carpet and then trying to shove it unrumpled across a rough floor.

The problem becomes much simpler if we imagine overthrust slabs moving downhill under the pull of gravity instead. In response to a push from behind, gravity exerts its force equally on every particle of rock in the slab so there is no need to think of a force pushing from behind. However that leaves unanswered the question of how an overthrust slab can move despite the enormous friction along the fault surface.

Some geologists argue that overthrust slabs could move almost without friction if the pore spaces in the rocks contained water under extremely high pressure. With those conditions, the water would help support the weight of the slab and greatly reduce friction along the fault surface and thus lubricate movement. However, many of the rocks in the overthrust belt contain very little pore space and that makes it difficult to imagine water could have played an important role in their movement.

Most geologists now suspect that overthrust fault movement probably involves slippage on the weaker bedrock. The thick layers of relatively strong rock such as limestone and sandstone seem to slide on beds of shale or mudstone as though they were on grease. In any case, it is clear that overthrust slabs must move with virtually no friction along the fault surface because they glide down extremely gentle slopes, and the rock near the fault surface shows little evidence of breakage.

DAVE ALT graduated in 1961 from the University of Texas with a PhD in Geology and came to the University of Montana in 1965 teaching Geology up until his retirement in 2003. He is the author of many popular roadside geology books including Roadside Geology of Montana and penned a book on Glacial Lake Missoula.

REGIONS OF BOB MARSHALL COUNTRY
by Rick and Susie Graetz

The physical attributes of the Bob Marshall country are more easily understood, if they are thought of by regions. The following land-form descriptions are generally based on river drainages. It would be extremely helpful to refer to the Bob Marshall Complex Map as it covers the entire Bob Marshall country including the Scapegoat and Great Bear Wilderness areas. You can get one at your local outdoor shop or contact Forest Service Ranger stations and Forest Supervisor offices in places near the Bob such as Great Falls, Kalispell and Missoula as well as the smaller communities.

The Rocky Mountain Front

Beyond the reach of recorded history, people migrating south from what is now Alaska into what became Montana established a passageway (now known as The Old North Trail) along the eastern flank of an imposing natural barrier. The first white travelers heading westward across the northern prairie gazed at glistening peaks ahead of them, a commanding sight they called the *shining mountains.* Today, we refer to this 120-mile north/south stretch of one of the most spectacular pieces of geography on the continent as the Rocky Mountain Front.

This is where the plains end and the mountains begin. No transition zone of slowly rising foothills ... the mountain wall wastes no space in making its presence felt. And what a presence! The spectacular mountains of The Front, rising 2,000 to 4,000 feet above the plains, are the gates to the wildlands beyond.

The softer side of the landscape flows to the east. Rippling rounded hills are interspersed with buttes, river bottoms, flatland, clusters of deciduous and conifer trees and wetlands. When coupled with the powerful massif that halts its sweep on the west, the blend is what has inspired people to love and cherish this place.

The Front is also alive and rich with wildlife, making a home for many species that have disappeared elsewhere. The largest population of grizzly bear and wolverine south of Canada roam here, along with sizable numbers of bighorn sheep. This is the only place in the lower 48 states where the big bears still venture out to the prairie they roamed when Lewis and Clark explored Montana. Gray wolves frequent the northern canyons of the Front. West slope cutthroat trout, for the most part found only west of the Continental Divide, inhabit some of the streams of the region. The reefs and soaring walls provide sanctuary for bald and golden eagles and both prairie and peregrine falcons. The southern reaches serve as wintering ground for the huge Sun River elk herd as well as deer and antelope.

Most insignificant of the inhabitants of the Front in relation to the space they occupy is the human species. Hard up against the rise of the mountains, widely separated ranches and a scattering of isolated houses dot the open expanse. A few structures have worked their way into the canyon openings. Otherwise, the immediate Rocky Mountain Front is free of extensive people presence. Even the towns, set well to the east of the mountains, are unobtrusive. They are pleasant, small communities: Augusta, Choteau, Bynum, Pendroy, Dupuyer, Heart Butte and East Glacier, spaced over 152 miles of highway.

To understand the infinite value of this majestic piece of our state, probe its roads and trails in all seasons. In the long light of a summer evening, watch as all the details of the heights slowly fade, leaving a purple silhouette on the horizon. Catch the rich first light of a rising sun on Castle Reef or Ear Mountain. In autumn, marvel at the delicate gold of the aspens and cottonwoods in the canyons of the Teton River. On a bright January day, from the high point of the highway between Augusta and Choteau, scan the white immensity of what lies before you. And on a late May or June evening, inhale the intoxicating aroma of wildflowers that blanket the undulating hills.

There are several good locations to access the Front. In the north, from Dupuyer on US 89, a route leads west to Swift Reservoir and the North and South Forks of Birch Creek, entryways to the Bob Marshall and Great Bear Wilderness areas. Seven miles north of Choteau, also on Hwy 89, a road heads toward the Front and the South and North Forks of the Teton River. The route splits just before the mountains, with one following the South Fork and the other the North Fork past Teton Pass Ski Area (try it next winter) to the West Fork of the Teton. As these roads penetrate deeper into the landscape than most others, it is an ideal place to experience the uniqueness of the area.

Augusta on US 287 provides easy entry into the southern Front. One byway goes west to the Sun River Canyon and Gibson Reservoir and another to Benchmark, a favorite horse route into the Bob. Highway 435 extending west and south of Augusta, points to Bean Lake and the Dearborn Canyon.

Two Medicine-Badger Creek-Heart Butte

The first region starts in the north and covers the land between Glacier Park's southern boundary and the North Fork of Birch Creek. While most of the Rocky Mountain Front consists of big peaks and deep canyons, this segment includes the broad glacial valley of the South Fork of the Two Medicine River. Most of the peaks are part of Two Medicine Ridge, and with the exception of those near Birch Creek, are lower and less rugged than the summits farther south.

Flowing north-northeast from the Continental Divide to the prairie is another major drainage. Two Medicine, which starts in a meadow between Kyo Crag and Bullshoe Mountain, also flows north-northeast. Both are part of the Marias River system and offer fair fishing.

Just north of the North Fork of Birch Creek, is an inviting grouping of peaks begging to be climbed, they are: 8,095-foot Family Peak, 8,282-foot Scarface Mountain, 8,376-foot Morningstar Mountain, 8,054-foot Spotted Eagle Mountain and 7,923-foot Curly Bear Mountain. These peaks are seldom visited, yet access is easy via the trail up Birch Creek from Swift Reservoir to Badger Pass and then down Badger Creek. The Badger Trail continues to Hwy 2.

Heart Butte on the edge of the Front is a prominent landmark that Indians once scaled to seek visions.

Birch Creek Country

The next geographical sector takes in the terrain from the North Fork of Birch Creek south to a divide that tops out at Corrugate Ridge on the Continental Divide, heading northeast over Mount Patrick Gass, Bloody Hill, Bennie Hill and Hurricane Mountain. The Continental Divide is its western boundary.

A popular hiking area owing to its varied and spectacular scenery and easy access from Swift Reservoir, the North, Middle and South Forks of Birch Creek drain the country. The canyons are narrow in most places, but easy to negotiate. The 8,625-foot Mount Patrick Gass, named after a member of the Lewis and Clark Expedition, is a great climb, and is approached by way of a pass up Crazy Creek, a tributary of the South Fork of Birch Creek. It may also be reached from the North Fork of the Teton and Bruce Creek to the south.

Two big walls hem in Swift Reservoir, Major Steele Backbone on the north and Walling Reef to the south.

Teton River Drainage

The region south of the Birch Creek country to a divide that runs between Rocky Mountain Peak and Ear Mountain offers perhaps the most diverse recreation, coupled with mountain splendor, on the Front. Here, the mountains are big and awesome, with great relief.

Two roads fork from the main road out of Choteau, one goes up the North Fork of the Teton River, ending near the confluence of the North and West Forks of the Teton, the other follows the South Fork of the Teton to the Headquarters Pass trailhead, both reach the wilderness buffer zone. The scenery en route is unparalleled and shows the best of the Rocky Mountain Front. Forest Service campgrounds are found at the end of each of these roads.

The North Fork Road is plowed in winter to Teton Pass ski area, a small gem of a ski mountain, owned and operated by a private group from Choteau. The scenery and the friendliness of the people make this a worthwhile place to visit. The remaining three miles of the road, down to the West Fork Ranger Station, remains unplowed and is set-aside as a snowmobile area, as are other places below the ski area.

Because of the plowed road, good ski touring is possible deep into the wilderness. This is probably the best possibility of high-country touring of any along the Front and west.

For the hiker and climber, the trail from the West Fork goes up to Teton Pass on the divide and opens up the headwaters country of the Middle Fork of the Flathead. Mount Patrick Gass, mentioned earlier, is reached from the West Fork, as is 8,855-foot Mount Wright.

The South Fork Road leads to one of the main routes into the Sun River country and the Chinese Wall, and the trail to Headquarters Pass. This trail is also the route to 9,392-foot Rocky Mountain Peak, the highest peak on the Rocky Mountain Front. By virtue of its elevation, this beautiful mountain reveals to the climber, much of the Bob Marshall country on all sides. The peaks of Glacier are visible way to the north as is the Swan Crest far to the west. And on a clear day, the outlying prairie ranges, some 100 miles away, come into view.

Teton Peak, 8,416 feet, another big Front apex is reached by the trail to 7,263-foot Route Creek Pass, or by a rugged cross-country walk from below Teton Pass ski area.

Ear Mountain, 8,380 feet, is the sentinel guarding the South Fork of the Teton Canyon and the Ear Mountain Game Range. It's a stiff but worthwhile climb. You reach the top via a gap on the west side.

Gibson Lake, Ford and Wood Creeks

The divide between Rocky Mountain Peak and Ear Mountain separates the Teton from the Deep Creek drainage and the next area of the Front. From this divide south to the road through Wood Canyon to Benchmark is another sector offering varied recreation, because of the presence of several roads and Gibson Lake. This country is reached out of Augusta.

The centerpiece is five-and-one-half-mile-long Gibson Reservoir — the Sun River impounded by Gibson Dam. Gibson is too cold for swimming but offers good boat fishing, especially in the spring. The road from Augusta goes to the lake near the dam and a Forest Service campground. A trail takes off from here into the wilderness through the canyons of the North and South Forks of the Sun.

The peaks and gulches on the north side of the lake serve as major winter range for a large bighorn sheep population, and whitetail deer and elk.

Deep Creek Canyon, to the north, is very scenic and impressive. Access is best gained by hiking the various gulches, with Blacktail offering the only through trail. Deep Creek flows to the prairie, but private ground and rough roads must be negotiated on the east.

A scenic road, open only part of the year, goes south from Gibson Dam up Beaver Creek, down Willow Creek and back to Augusta. From the same road, west of Augusta, another road heads to Benchmark Ranger Station through Ford and Wood Creek Canyons.

Benchmark is perhaps the most heavily used trailhead into the Bob Marshall Wilderness, especially by horse parties. Trails from here also lead to the Scapegoat Wilderness. The way up the South Fork of the Sun and the West Fork of the South Fork is a good route to White River Pass and the Chinese Wall. Packers also use it to reach the White River and the South Fork of the Flathead.

Renshaw Mountain, 8,264 feet, is reached by trail from the Benchmark area, and 8,245-foot Fairview Mountain from the Beaver-Willow Creek Road, both are good climbs. Both peaks give the hiker an excellent perspective on the overthrust geology of the area. The view defines definite north-south alignment of the long gulches and shows off the sheer east faces and sloping west sides of the reefs and ridges.

Sawtooth Ridge, 8,175 feet, and Castle Reef, 7,005 feet, on the north and south sides of the Sun, are the gates to the Sun River Canyon. The Sun River Game Range, wintering grounds for a large elk herd, is below the east wall of Sawtooth.

Dearborn River-Falls Creek

The southern-most segment of the Rocky Mountain Front takes in the country between the Wood-Ford Creek Road south to the Continental Divide and Lewis and Clark Pass. The Continental Divide borders it on the west. Roads from Augusta up Smith Creek and Elk Creek, and the Dearborn River from a road off of Hwy 200, provide access.

The Smith Creek and Elk Creek roads lead to Scapegoat Wilderness trailheads. The base of 6,004-foot Elk Pass, a few miles from the end of the Elk Creek Road, is the take-off point for a trail to the top of 8,579-foot Steamboat Mountain. For a view of most of the Rocky Mountain Front and the wilderness, this spot offers the best of any. It is farther east than the other peaks and reefs of the Front, enabling the climber to see the collision point of the prairie and mountains.

The Dearborn Road ends at a church camp several miles to the west of Bean Lake. From here, the trail follows the river to the Welcome Creek area and eventually to the Dearborn headwaters below Scapegoat Mountain.

The country to the south of the Dearborn is called the Falls Creek-Silver King area. Trails lead in from the Dearborn Road and from Lewis and Clark Pass. Caribou Peak, 8,773 feet, on the Continental Divide is at the head of the several forks of Falls Creek.

We've covered the Rocky Mountain Front in more detail than the other geographic regions of the Bob Marshall country for several reasons. First, it is our favorite place of all the wild country we've ever been privileged to see.

The combination of beautiful rolling prairie, sheer mountain majesty, awesome canyons and such a wide expanse is unsurpassed. The roads that venture into the canyons give those who aren't able to, or choose not to, ride horseback or walk, the opportunity to see all that the wilderness traveler observes. It gives these people a touch of wildness on a grand scale. If formal wilderness designation comes to the wild lands near and beyond these roads, the roads will remain open, and what the visitor sees will be further enhanced.

The only way we can improve on what we see now from the roads and trails is to design the areas deserving of it, wilderness status. Some of the ranchers in the area would like to see the country remain as is, without wilderness protection. That would be perfectly desirable except that administrations in Washington and in the Forest Service change and, we can't be assured of protection forever. It must be emphasized, that any gas potential or timber value is minuscule compared to the value that wildness gives to the country, both in real economic terms and multiple-use values of recreation, watershed protection, wild habitat and grazing.

And indeed the country in a wild state is valuable. Montana sportsmen have helped increase the wildlife population of the Front with the purchase of three game ranges: the Sun River Range west of Augusta near the mouth of the Sun River Canyon, Ear Mountain Game Range west of Choteau and just south of the South Fork of the Teton Canyon, and Blackleaf Game Range west of Bynum by the mouth of Blackleaf Canyon.

Thanks to these efforts, and those of the ranchers along the Front, the elk population is ten times greater, and the mule deer herd 20 times larger than at the turn of the 20th century, and the bighorn sheep population is a national resource.

To further enhance wildlife habitat on the Front, The Nature Conservancy of Montana, began in 1978 to assemble one of the largest and most stunning of its sanctuary projects, the Pine Butte Swamp Preserve. Using carefully assembled biological data, The Conservancy has identified for protection some 50,000 acres of foothills, prairie, swamp and river floodplain. Keying its project on the threatened grizzly bear, The Conservancy saved the last regularly used prairie habitat for the great bear. In the course of that protection effort, essential habitat for many other species of plants and animals will be secure for generations to come.

Recognizing that the task of protecting the Front Range necessitates combined private and public action, The Conservancy works with ranchers, public- and private-interest organizations, state and federal agencies to find agreeable mixes of land ownership, use and management for the Front Range. The success of the Pine Butte Swamp project bodes well for similar efforts all along the Front. Ideally, The Nature Conservancy approach could result in effective noncontroversial protection for key lands from Canada to Hwy 200. Committed to helping keep the local ranchers on their lands, the intermingled private and public land holdings arranged capably and intelligently would then complement the wild land and wildlife values that are now exposed to a host of development threats.

Sun River Drainages

The North Fork of the Sun, headwatering at 7,800 feet Sun River Pass on the Continental Divide, drains a portion of the west side of the Rocky Mountain Front and the mass of mountains just to the east of the divide between Sun River Pass and Gibson Lake.

Incidentally, Sun River Pass separates the Sun drainage from that of the Middle Fork of the Flathead. It is 30 miles from the pass to where the North Fork enters Gibson Lake.

Timber is heavier and open spaces scarce in the upper reaches of the North Fork. As one travels south, meadows and extensive parks become more prevalent. Gates Park (formerly called Cates after an early day homesteader) is the first significant exposed stretch. It is the site of a Forest Service backcountry guard station and presents good views of the surrounding mountains. The valley of the North Fork, perhaps the widest in the Bob Marshall country, begins to spread out here. Below Gates Park, the timber returns, but soon other meadows such as Biggs Creek Flat, Two Shacks Flat and Circle Creek are reached. Before wilderness designation, cattle grazed these areas. Now with the cattle gone, trees are closing in on the smaller parks. Recent fires have spurred growth of replacement trees.

From Circle Creek south, there are few trees in the bottomlands and on the slopes to the east. This region is habitat, to within a couple of miles north of Gibson Lake, for the big Sun River elk herd.

The mountains on the west side of the Sun River, all the way across to the West Fork of the South Fork of the Sun and the Continental Divide, are part of the Sun River Game Preserve. No hunting is allowed in the preserve. Many times we have trekked through the country, either on skis or foot, and witnessed herds of elk stampeding all around us to cross the river to the game preserve where they knew they'd be safe.

Big Salmon Lake at its outlet in what was then the South Fork of the Flathead Primitive Area when this photo was taken in 1934. K.D.SWAN/U.S. FOREST SERVICE

From the North Fork Valley and Elk Ridge, several impressive mountain peaks may be seen, including Scapegoat Mountain, Sheep Mountain, and Prairie Reef. To climb Scapegoat, it is necessary to trek cross-country, but a trail goes to the top of Prairie Reef from the West Fork of the Sun. It's a tough six miles, but for the views it offers of the Chinese Wall, the Sun River country and the Rocky Mountain Front to the east, it's worth it.

Two well-used trails start out of the North Fork of the Sun country heading to the Chinese Wall. From Gates Park, a trail runs up Hoxsey and Rock creeks to Spotted Bear Pass then over to Larch Hill Pass and the northern end of the wall. From Two Shacks Flat, the Moose Creek Trail goes directly to the center section of the wall. This is a favorite horsepacker route. Just above the head of Gibson Lake and the confluence of the North and South Forks of the Sun River is Medicine Springs. The Klick family has an inholding here for a guest ranch and the spring is now used for their guests, but at one time, Indians traveled to this area to use the water for healing purposes. Hence the name, Medicine Springs.

The mass of mountains south of Moose Creek and on the west side of the North Fork of the Sun separates this drainage from that of the West Fork of the South Fork of the Sun. The West Fork begins in a small, swampy lake below an outlying ridge of the Chinese Wall near Cliff Mountain, the highest point on the Wall. From here, it tumbles down a narrow steep canyon on its 13-mile journey to the confluence of the South Fork of the Sun. Below Indian Point, the site of a Forest Service Guard Station, the river is an intermittent mix of open meadows and forest. Trails from the West Fork, in the vicinity of Indian Point, lead to White River Pass and the south end of the Chinese Wall, as well as to Pearl Basin on the Continental Divide.

The South Fork of the Sun River has its headwaters near Scapegoat Mountain at 8,500 feet on the Continental Divide. As it flows on its 25-mile journey to Gibson Lake, it passes Benchmark, a U.S. Forest Service work site and trailhead — one of the more popular routes into the Bob Marshall country. For the most part, the canyon is timbered and rocky, but downstream from its confluence with the West Fork is Pretty Prairie, a series of big meadows.

From Benchmark, a trail works its way up the South Fork of the Sun into the Scapegoat country and 9,790-foot Flint Mountain. This same trail is a good route into the Danaher Meadows on the west side of the Continental Divide. It winds over some of the high points of the Scapegoat Plateau. Another route from this trail goes over 7,444-foot Observation Pass into the Danaher.

Continental Divide Ranges

From the north, the Continental Divide commences its journey into the heart of the Bob Marshall country at 5,206-foot Marias Pass. At this point on Glacier National Park's southern border, no road will again cross the Divide for more than 145 miles until it reaches 5,609-foot Rogers Pass and Montana Hwy 200. An unofficial Continental Divide Trail stays with the divide for about 168 miles. In many areas, especially the southern end, bushwhacking is required. Forest Service maps, USGS guides and inquiries to local Forest Service offices would help in planning a Divide trek.

The peaks along the Divide aren't the highest in the wilderness complex. In the northern third of the area the highest points are 8,590-foot Mount Field near Badger Pass, and 8,412-foot Kevan Mountain near Switchback Pass and Dean Lake. Along the central Divide, the highest elevations are 8,310-foot Hahn Peak on what is called the north wall; 8,789-foot Redhead Peak east of Spotted Bear Pass; 8,576-foot Cliff Mountain and 8,396-foot Haystack Mountain, the two highest points on the Chinese Wall; 8,700-foot Junction Mountain in the Flathead Alps and above Pearl Basin; and 8,744-foot Twin Peaks above Ahorn Basin. On the southern crest the tallest summits are 8,698-foot Sugarloaf north of Observation Pass; 8,572-foot Triple Divide; 8,523-foot Observation Point; 9,079-foot Flint Mountain and 9,204-foot Scapegoat Mountain. The latter four are part of the Scapegoat massif. In the Lincoln backcountry, 8,611-foot Crow Peak above Carmichael Basin and 8,773-foot Caribou Peak are the tallest pinnacles.

Some of the Bob's most prominent features straddle the Continental Divide. Big River Meadows is one of these, so named because Gateway Creek begins here as one of the headwater streams of the big Middle Fork of the Flathead. These huge fields offer a rare place where you walk into a mountain pass, rather than climb up to it. Gateway Pass, a favorite Indian route across the Continental Divide, is at the eastern edge of the meadows.

West of Big River Meadows, Strawberry Creek, starting out as a spring at Badger Pass on the Divide, joins with Gateway Creek to help form the Middle Fork of the Flathead.

The Big River Meadows, Gateway and Badger passes are reached by trails up the North and South Forks of Birch Creek from Swift Reservoir.

Corrugate Ridge, a four-mile-long limestone wall, is another Divide landmark, and reached byway of Teton Pass or Bruce Creek from the road's end at the West Fork Teton Station.

The Kevan Mountain-Switchback Pass area of the Continental Divide, deep in the wilderness, is very impressive and is attained by a hard walk from the West Fork Teton and Birch Creek trails or from Spotted Bear on the South Fork of the Flathead.

A trip to the *piece de resistance* of the Bob Marshall, the Chinese Wall, is for some, whether on foot or by horse, a lifetime goal. And why not … the landscape is legendary in the annals of backcountry lore and in a state that boasts of some of the most the magnificent topography on the planet, this escarpment is outstanding!

With its sheer east cliff and gradual westward down slope, the Chinese Wall is the epitome of classic overthrusting. Geologically speaking, it is part of the overthrust belt, a massive formation (Montana's segment reaches from north of Helena to the Canadian border) consisting of a series of monumental slabs of older rocks that were tilted upwards and then pushed eastward to cover younger horizontal layers of sedimentary rocks. The Rocky Mountain Front is the eastern most periphery of the belt and the Chinese Wall the most visible western expansion.

From a plane heading toward the sunset while crossing the Bob, there is no mistaking the Chinese Wall — amidst a labyrinth of other scarps and mountains it majestically shows its face. From any high point to its east, the first thing many climbers exclaim upon reaching the top is "*look there's the Chinese Wall.*"

Viewing it up close is an inspiring experience — it's a place unto its own. The Continental Divide defines its 13-mile-long crest and rather than forming a simple straight wall, it creates a series of half moon-like basins, each with its own character, along its entire length.

From the wildflower-filled meadows at its base, there is as much as a 1,000-foot immediate gain in elevation to the top of the Wall. The western surface slopes gradually for three to four miles down to the White River.

Eagles, hawks and other birds of prey find resting places in its nooks, crannies and small shelves. Mountain goats commonly found on some of the steepest terrain, are restricted to the north and south ends as well as "*Trick Pass*" in its mid-section. You need flying capabilities to perch on this piece of geography.

For humans, the Continental Divide Trail, with its roller coaster-like profile, skirts the Wall on the east. A backcountry traveler can get close enough to touch the Chinese Wall for about six miles. On the south, the trail ascends Burnt Creek, one of the flows that create the West Fork of the Sun River, to a pass just below 8,576-foot

Cliff Mountain, the highest pinnacle atop the wall. From here, much of the extent of the Chinese Wall makes its presence visible. The way then drops quickly northward to the head of Moose Creek underneath 8,270-foot Salt Mountain, another lofty point on these limestone cliffs. This is the area of Trick Pass a somewhat hidden goat route, and the only place where a hiker can ascend the Wall mid-way along its length.

After several ups and downs, the route along the base climbs to 7,702-foot Larch Hill Pass and the Wall's northern terminus and another viewpoint and access place to the top.

A windswept saddle, White River Pass, at 7,590 feet, crosses the Continental Divide and Chinese Wall near its southern conclusion, but it's the Cliff Mountain and Larch Hill passes that present the pre-eminent panoramas.

As should be the case, it's a fair distance from the fringes of Bob Marshall country into the Wall. Trails access this landmark from all compass points, but the best approaches are from the Rocky Mountain Front and Spotted Bear.

From Benchmark, west of Augusta, it's about 23 miles to Cliff Mountain. Crossing Headquarters Pass west of Choteau via Gates Park to Larch Hill Pass, 27 miles are covered. Following Gibson Lake from the Sun River Canyon and then trails edging the North Fork of the Sun River and Moose Creek, 26 miles need to be negotiated.

A point-to-point route starts at Spotted Bear, south of Hungry Horse, and exits at Benchmark 46 miles away. This trail reaches the Wall at Larch Hill Pass and parallels it to Cliff Mountain.

Fortunately, the U.S. Forest Service, the agency responsible for managing the Bob Marshall complex (the contiguous Bob Marshall, Scapegoat and Great Bear wilderness areas), prohibits camping below the Wall and thus the landscape is pristine and untouched for all to enjoy.

A close second to the Chinese Wall as a spectacular geologic masterpiece is the Scapegoat Mountain complex. At 9,204 feet, Scapegoat Mountain is the highest peak in the Bob Marshall country sector of the Continental Divide. The mountain itself is only a big bump on top of a three- to four-mile-long limestone plateau. The walls are sheer on almost all sides with access to the top restricted to the Green Fork drainage on the east and a few places on the west side. The top of the plateau is somewhat flat and then rises on the north to 9,079-foot Flint Mountain.

The entire massif is honeycombed with caves and is a favorite of serious cavers. In the Green Fork drainage, a stream pours out of the wall like a faucet, and behind it is a cave reported to be about two miles long. A word of warning is necessary here: These caves are not for amateurs to explore; they are dangerous.

Half Moon Park, below the northeast side of Scapegoat Mountain, is an unbelievable place; and since a fire has burned through the area, it is open to all views. Below a ridge to the south of Half Moon, the Dearborn River begins flowing to the prairie and the Missouri River.

Access to the Scapegoat is usually from the east by way of Elk Pass, the Dearborn River, Smith Creek or the Benchmark area. From the south and west side, approaches to the Scapegoat Mountain and Plateau are from the Danaher, the North Fork of the Blackfoot River and the Lincoln backcountry. The Dobroda Creek headwater area, reached by trail from the North Fork Blackfoot Valley, offers one of the better ways to climb Scapegoat from the west.

Many passes cross the Continental Divide Range. Some of them are: Muskrat Pass, 5,974 feet, coming up from the Badger Creek and the Two Medicine River drainage to Beaver Lake; 6,278-foot Badger Pass and the Middle Fork of the Flathead headwaters; Gateway Pass, 6,478 feet, an historic pass used by the Indians crossing from the west to the buffalo hunting grounds, reached by going up the South Fork of Birch Creek or from the Middle Fork country; Teton Pass, 7,775 feet, reached from the West Fork Teton River and leading to Bowl Creek and the Middle Fork of the Flathead; Switchback Pass, 7,767 feet, on the divide between the Spotted Bear River and Sun River headwaters; Spotted Bear Pass, 6,721 feet, reached by way of Rock Creek to the east and the Spotted Bear River on the north side; Larch Hill Pass, 7,702 feet, the north end of the Chinese Wall; White River Pass, 7,626 feet, the southern end of the wall and part of a major route across the Bob; Camp Creek Pass, 7,200 feet, reached from the Danaher and providing access to Pearl Basin; Observation Pass, 7,444 feet, a crossing from the South Fork of the Sun to the upper Danaher Basin. South of Scapegoat Mountain, a few trails traverse the Divide on lower, unnamed passes.

The Continental Divide Range is for the most part seldom visited along most of its route. Peak and pass elevations and locations have been listed to provide points of reference. To see it in these areas requires bushwhacking and some steep climbing. If you are in shape, have good equipment, know how to use a GPS, map and compass, and know what you are doing, the rewards are well worth the effort.

This is pristine country. Practice no-trace camping and remember much of the area provides a summer sanctuary for wildlife.

The Middle Fork of the Flathead Drainage

Old timers called Montana's wildest waterway *"Big River."* Today it is known as the Middle Fork of the Flathead. Indeed it is big; the river and its tributaries dominate the Great Bear Wilderness. The drainage basin is bordered on the east and parts of the south by the Continental Divide and Elk Ridge, some high country near Pentagon Mountain. The Flathead Range flanks the west and the southern boundary, and Glacier Park, the north.

The big river begins its journey at the confluence of Strawberry and Bowl Creeks and flows for 46 miles through the wilderness to Bear Creek at Hwy 2. For its first 15 miles, it is in a very remote timbered valley before reaching Schafer Meadows. Featuring a landing strip that has been kept open as part of an agreement struck when the Great Bear Wilderness was created, Schafer is somewhat of an island in the wilderness. From here north, the stream cuts through sedimentary rock cliffs that climb to steep mountain slopes above. En route, it varies between wild and often dangerous waters to calm pools.

This stretch from Schafer downstream, offers some of the best and most spectacular whitewater floating in Montana. A segment somewhere between three to four miles long, below Spruce Park, is a favorite of whitewater enthusiasts. In this area alone, the river drops more than 40 feet per mile. The Middle Fork in its entirety offers the steepest drop per mile of any of the forks of the Flathead River. It starts at 5,500 feet at Strawberry Creek and falls to 3,800 feet at Bear Creek. Its average drop is 35 feet per mile in the wilderness stretch, compared to 15 feet for the North Fork and 19 feet for the South Fork of the Flathead. (These figures come from an outstanding book, *Great Bear, Wild River* by Dale A Burk.)

The conditions for floating are best in May and June, and sometimes, early July. That is, if you like your water fast, as this is the peak of the runoff season. It is best to check conditions with the U.S. Forest Service for the time you plan to go.

Fishing on the Middle Fork is better the farther you get from Schafer Meadows. Easy access to the area has virtually destroyed the fishing there.

Many tributaries add to the flow of the Middle Fork, but some are especially noteworthy. Gateway Creek originates in the Big River Meadows just off the Continental Divide and flows through Gateway Gorge, a towering limestone wall created by water and wind erosion that rises more than 1,000 feet above the stream. Gateway eventually joins Strawberry Creek, which starts as a trickle just below Badger Pass on the Continental Divide.

Bowl Creek starts on the Continental Divide at Teton Pass and rushes down a steep canyon to join Strawberry Creek, forming the Middle Fork. It is reached byway of the West Fork of the Teton over Teton Pass and also from the trails coming down Strawberry Creek.

Commencing at Dean and Trilobite lakes, Clack Creek travels through some of the Bob's most scenic country. The Trilobite Range, high above this stream, is a massive landform that vies with the river itself for attention. Running the full stretch of the Clack and Dean creek drainage as those waters make their way to the Middle Fork of the Flathead at Gooseberry Park, the range, starting just above Dean Lake, was named after the fossils found in it. The 8,877-foot Pentagon Mountain, one of the most beautiful summits in the Bob Marshall country, is at the southern tip of the range. The range, or ridge, heads north until it runs out at Schafer Meadows, ten miles away.

Basin Creek, heading just below Pentagon Mountain, is part of the Middle Fork of the Flathead drainage, but it flows east before joining Bowl Creek and running north to the main river. Do not believe the maps that show a trail up it, because no trail exists, except in the lower portions. We have hiked the area several times, but the traces of the trail are very few and the going can be quite rough. And, it is grizzly country.

Dolly Varden Creek, named after the fish found in it, is on the west side of the Trilobite Range with its headwaters below Elk Ridge and Pentagon Mountain. The open sections in this country and some of the others on the east side of the Trilobite Range are an exception; for the most part, the headwaters country of the Middle Fork and its tributaries is heavily timbered.

Downstream from Schafer Meadows, the creeks coming in add to the water supply, but they are in more heavily timbered regions than those on the south and aren't as long as the upper streams.

The main Middle Fork's upper reaches are accessed by the trails just mentioned. However, the Big River Trail follows the entire length of the river to Hwy 2. In quite a few places it is well above the river, high up on the cliffs, opening up some great views of the canyon. Access to the lower segments of the river is gained via Granite Creek from a road off of Hwy 2 and Morrison Creek, reached by the same road.

All of the Middle Fork drainage is very mountainous, but most of the peaks are less than 8,000 feet high. However, as the river elevations decrease, the peaks become more imposing because of the greater relief.

It is important to note that much of the high country in the upper reaches of the Middle Fork of the Flathead and Great Bear Wilderness Region is very wild and remote and provides habitat for the great grizzly bear. It's something to keep in mind when traveling here.

The Central Ranges

This area, like the Chinese Wall, is the heart of the Bob Marshall country. It takes in the Spotted Bear drainage, just to the south of the Flathead Range, and is bordered by the Chinese Wall to the east and the South Fork of the Flathead River on the west. Culminating at Camp Creek Pass on the Continental Divide, south of the Chinese Wall, it also includes the country of the White River.

The Spotted Bear River starts on the Continental Divide below Spotted Bear Pass and is fed by several other notable tributaries including Wall and Silvertip creeks, whose headwaters are below Silvertip Mountain. The Wall Creek Cliffs in the headwaters area of the Spotted Bear are an interesting geologic formation and are nearly as high as the Chinese Wall, and also a jagged reef. Bungalow Mountain (8,140 feet) near the Wall Creek Cliffs is a good climb by trail from the same headwaters area, and is visited by few.

Silvertip Mountain (8,890 feet), just to the west of the Wall Creek Cliffs, is considered by many to be the sentinel of the Bob Marshall country. Visible from almost any point in this big wilderness complex, it is a favorite of cavers and is reported to contain one of the deepest caves in the United States as well as more than five miles of lateral caves. The Silvertip area, named after one of the grizzly bear's nicknames, provides excellent summer bear habitat.

The White River, a major tributary of the South Fork of the Flathead, is born on the west slopes of Silvertip Mountain. The drainage is hemmed in on the west by a ridge of peaks going south from Silvertip Peak and by the Wall Creek Cliffs and the Larch Hill Pass ridge coming off of the south end of the Chinese Wall, and the Wall itself to the east. It's a very definite basin that shows evidence a glacier had started in a cirque below Silvertip Mountain and carved out a perfect U-shaped valley for much of the White River's route. The sloping west side of the Chinese Wall begins its rise from the White River bottomlands. From below Silvertip Mountain the shallow and wide White River flows for 20 miles on its way to the South Fork of the Flathead. Initially, it runs south and then turns west. The smaller South Fork of the White River joins the main stream just below White River Pass and the southern end of the Chinese Wall. This lower end of the river follows along one of the major routes crossing the Bob Marshall.

Geologically, the upper valley of the White River is unusual compared to most of the Bob Marshall country, because of a phenomenon called the White River Syncline. Here, the east slope of the mountains above the river's west side drops gently westward, whereas in most of the Bob, the peaks and ridges rise sharply on the east and gradually on the west. The lower White River up to Needle Falls provides excellent fishing. Some of the upper stretches are good for portions of the year, but tend to dry up later in the summer. The group of mountains above the White River to the west offers an alternate route to the South Fork of the Flathead via a trail over The falls serves as a fish barrier. Pagoda Pass on the south side of 8.030-foot Pagoda Mountain. The main trail goes down Helen Creek. A cross-country route above Damnation Creek, with a trail visible part of the way, could be followed with difficulty.

Pagoda is a good climb as are 8,804-foot Helen Mountain and 8,483-foot Lone Butte. The slopes of these peaks, as well as much of the upper parts of the White River country, are open. Excellent views are the rule.

The rugged and glacier-scoured peaks towering over the White River to the south are called the Flathead Alps. These mountains are some of the most spectacular in the Bob Marshall country. Junction Mountain, 8,700 feet, on the Continental Divide is the highest in the range. All the other peaks are less than 8,000 feet, but as seen from the South Fork of the Flathead, they rise several thousand feet. Trails meander to them from the South Fork and the Danaher. Although they may be somewhat accessible from the White River Trail, they are best reached from the South Fork drainage or by way of Pearl Basin and Camp Creek Pass, coming up from the West Fork of the South Fork of the Sun River.

Like many of the other high remote areas of the Bob Marshall country, this too is prime grizzly habitat. For your safety and out of respect for the bear, if you wish to wander in these high remote places, consider that this is his home. Plan to visit some of these areas in the winter or earlier in the year when the bear may be feeding at lower altitudes.

Caribou Peak (bottom) in the Scapegoat Country. U.S. FOREST SERVICE PHOTO

Flathead Range-Hungry Horse Lake Area

This region is bordered on the east by the Middle Fork of the Flathead drainage and on the west by the Swan Range and the west shore of Hungry Horse Lake. U.S. Hwy 2 and Glacier Park border it on the north and the Spotted Bear River to the south.

The peaks of the Flathead Range, like many in the northern part of the Bob Marshall country, look much higher than they really are. Most are less than 8,000 feet, yet the relief in the area is more than 4,000 feet.

From Hungry Horse Lake, and also from parts of Hwy 2, the two highest peaks, 8,705-foot Great Northern Mountain and 8,590-foot Mount Grant, are clearly visible. Close to each other and not all that far from roads, these are very tough climbs.

The best access to Great Northern Mountain is from the logging roads on the west side. This is the only safe way it can be climbed in the winter. Check with the Hungry Horse Ranger Station for details. A more scenic route for summer use is up Stanton Creek by way of picturesque Stanton Lake. However, the trail disappears in the upper parts and it is necessary to negotiate very steep, brush-infested avalanche slopes. After leaving the brush, the climber faces precipitous rocky slopes to negotiate before reaching a glacier on the northeast side of the mountain.

Mount Grant is accessed by Grant Creek from Hwy 2.

There are other peaks in the Flathead Range, but they aren't as easily reached and it is necessary to do quite a bit of cross-country walking and bushwhacking.

Hungry Horse Reservoir is not a wilderness body of water as it is circumvented by a road and surrounded by many clear cuts. However, it is still part of the Bob Marshall and provides access to the backcountry. The lake was formed in 1953, when the South Fork of the Flathead River was dammed for a flood control project.

The lake is 34 miles long and three to four miles across at its widest. Boating is popular, but stumps found in the bays and near the islands can be hazardous. For this reason, and because of the cold water temperature, swimming and water skiing are not favored here.

Narrow, winding gravel roads follow both shorelines; travel is slow at best. However, the roads reach several campgrounds, places to put a boat in and to enjoy various scenic views for those who can ignore the clear-cuts on the slopes. In spite of these shortcomings, Hungry Horse Lake is well worth seeing. These roads also lead to the Spotted Bear Work Center and Ranger Station, a Forest Service complex. From the complex, another road leads to Beaver Creek Campground and trails into the Spotted Bear River headwaters. Off the route to Spotted Bear, a road leads to Meadow and Bunker creeks where trails head toward the South Fork of the Flathead, and beyond.

For more information on Hungry Horse Lake and boating possibilities, an address appears elsewhere in this book. Access is by way of Hungry Horse located on Hwy 2 near the entrance to Glacier National Park at West Glacier. Roads along the lake are open only in the summer months.

The Danaher and the South Fork of the Flathead

Streaming for more than 70 miles, the Danaher and the South Fork of the Flathead drain much of the western sector of the Bob Marshall country. This river system is an incomparable experience for many people. Outfitters use it to make a living, and backpackers, horse parties, fly fishermen and floaters enjoy all this wild, wilderness river offers. Everything is excellent in this tranquil setting. The waterway begins on the lowest pass in the Bob Marshall country, the Dry Fork Flathead Divide at 5,400 feet and just below 8,002-foot Danaher Mountain. For five to seven miles, the Danaher flows through timbered country until it starts meandering through broad meadows. The Danaher Meadows are the largest of these open areas. This was the site of an unsuccessful homesteading attempt before wilderness designation. Three miles north of the Danaher Meadows, the river enters what is simply called The Basin. Here Basin and Camp creeks come together with the Danaher. This was the site of an Indian battle over hunting rights.

After The Basin, the river pours through a canyon where it meets Youngs Creek. Here, Youngs Creek and the Danaher form the South Fork of the Flathead River. Along these upper stretches, there are many wide, grassy parks, some dotted with yellow pine and stately ponderosa. The first of these parks is at Big Prairie, the site of a Forest Service work center. Next come White River Park and Murphy Flats in the vicinity of where the White River enters the South Fork. Salmon Forks is several river miles downstream from Murphy Flats. Here, Big Salmon Creek, the outlet of Big Salmon Lake, meets the river. Farther downstream are Little Salmon Park and Black Bear Meadows. After Black Bear, the South Fork Canyon becomes much narrower, deeper and more heavily timbered.

Most of the tributary waters of the South Fork of the Flathead come in from the east slopes of the Swan Range — the best-known of these are Hahn, Youngs and Gordon creeks, which join the Flathead drainage in the Danaher region. Just a few miles below the start of the South Fork, Gordon Creek reaches the South Fork Valley. Youngs and Hahn creek drainages, with their many meadows, are very scenic in their lower reaches. Gordon Pass is a major route into this region by way of the Holland Lake country and the Swan Range. The White River comes in from the east farther downriver, as does Black Bear Creek. Bunker Creek and the Spotted Bear River join in where the river leaves the wilderness. Big Salmon Lake, just upstream from where Big Salmon Creek meets the South Fork, is a mountain gem. It's about four-and-a-half miles long and one-half mile wide, and sits 20 miles from Holland Lake in the Swan Valley and about another 20 miles from the Spotted Bear area.

There are many other less well-known drainages and trails that offer scenic surprises. The Picture Ridge Trail is such a spot. It is on the west slopes above the South Fork of the Flathead and not very far from the Spotted Bear country. It reaches its highest elevation at 7,729-foot Picture Point. The trail starts at the Bunker Creek Road and comes out at the Black Bear Guard Station on the river. When hiking this trail, especially late in the summer or fall, be sure to fill your water bottles whenever you have a chance.

There are several Forest Service backcountry guard stations found throughout the South Fork of the Flathead, as well as in other parts of the Bob. These are, for the most part, simple cabins often hidden from view that the Forest Service uses for administrative purposes, especially during the hunting season. They are not for public use. Occasionally, you'll see the ruins of other cabins used by early-day trappers in the South Fork.

Bunker Creek is another major drainage reaching the South Fork outside the wilderness. It has been described as *"The Valley of the Moon without the aesthetics."* A visit to this logged-over area will show you why.

As mentioned earlier, the South Fork is popular for floating. For the most part the waters are moderate, but there are some dangerous areas. Floaters often have outfitters or friends with horses pack their rafts to various points along the river and leave their cars south of Hungry Horse Reservoir. For those going all the way to the reservoir, a three-mile portage is required around an impassable gorge near the mouth of Bunker Creek. For more information, the Forest Service puts out a special brochure on the three forks of the Flathead River. It contains vital information for floaters.

Bruce Creek - Rocky Mountain Front.   RICK AND SUSIE GRAETZ

The Southern Mountains and Lincoln Backcountry

This region covers the country on the west from Montour Creek to Danaher Mountain, and eastward to Rogers Pass and the Continental Divide. Its northern boundary is a divide that runs along the crest of the range from Danaher Mountain to the Falls Creek country on the Rocky Mountain Front.

Smaller than other regions in the Bob, it makes up for size in its wild beauty. Highway 200 through the Blackfoot Valley provides excellent access via many secondary and gravel roads. Starting on the west side, trails lead out of Montour Creek toward Camp Pass and several smaller lakes on the south side of the Dry Fork Flathead Divide. Camp Lake, Lake Otatsy and Canyon Lake are small mountain lakes in a forested setting. Another trail leads to the canyon of the North Fork of the Blackfoot River and into the Scapegoat Wilderness.

Several mountain peaks in this western sector are worth climbing. Especially interesting are 8,351-foot Lake Mountain and 7,901-foot East Spread Mountain. Both afford panoramas of much of the Scapegoat Wilderness and the country to the south. Other roads and trails from this North Fork of the Blackfoot country lead into the Scapegoat via Meadow Lake and Meadow Creek. From here, there are many routes to take. One good possibility would be to start in the North Fork of the Blackfoot Canyon, going by way of the North Fork Cabin, and then head southeast along the east fork of the Blackfoot past the Meadow Lake Trail to Parker-Webb and Hart lakes. Side trails lead to the Continental Divide in the vicinity of Caribou Peak and Big Horn Lake. From Hart Lake you can walk the five miles out to the Copper Creek Campground. You can arrange to leave a car here for the ride back to Lincoln or take your chance on hitchhiking.

The Lincoln Backcountry is very accessible by way of the many logging and other gravel roads out of the town of Lincoln. Both a winter and summer playground, much of this country is getting to be a favorite destination in the higher reaches for skiers and in the lower valleys for snowmobilers.

At 9,411 feet, Red Mountain, the highest summit in the Bob Marshall country, is easily reached from the Lincoln area via logging roads or by trails from Hart Lake. The 7,771-foot Silver King Mountain in the Alice Creek area east of Lincoln also has easy access. Roads penetrate well into the valley of Alice Creek.

There are many facilities in the town of Lincoln, a mountain community that bills itself as a gateway to the wilderness.

For newcomers to the wilderness camping experiences, perhaps the Lincoln Backcountry and the regions of the North Fork of the Blackfoot River offer excellent grounds for short journeys.

The Swan Range

The Swan Range provides a majestic western boundary for the Bob Marshall country. Certainly this range would have to be considered one of the most beautiful in Montana. Besides guarding the Bob Marshall Wilderness, it presides over the impressive Swan Valley.

The crest of the range forms the western boundary of much of the Bob Marshall Wilderness. However, since this book is about the entire Bob Marshall country, the Swan Range is included because much of its west face is unroaded wild country deserving of wilderness status. Indeed, it is part of this entire eco-system.

For purposes of defining the Swan Range as a region within the Bob Marshall country, one can consider it to run from 7,234-foot Columbia Mountain on the north, a peak just south of the town of Columbia Falls, for approximately 130 miles to 8,062-foot Danaher Mountain and the start of the drainage of the South Fork of the Flathead. This distance is measured along the crest.

The northern 50 miles of the Swan Range crest are not within the wilderness area. Parts of it, especially the east slopes coming out of Hungry Horse Lake, are heavily logged.

The west side, because of its steepness and unstable soils, has fewer roads. Trails run along the crest of the range out of Columbia Falls.

Approximately mid-way is an island of wild country, the Jewel Basin Hiking Area, and what a gem it is. The Basin is accessible from the Echo Lake region in the Swan Valley or from the Hungry Horse Lake side. There are at least 28 beautiful lakes within these 15,349 acres of high mountain country. The Jewel Basin Hiking Area is a specially designated Backcountry Use Area. Elevations range from 7,530-foot Mount Aeneas, to a low point of 4,240 feet at Graves Creek. Here we have another example of low mountains with great relief. Special maps of the Jewel Basin area are available through the Forest Service.

From the southern end of Swan Lake, and from Swan Village, a trail leads to 7,406-foot Sixmile Mountain on the Swan divide. From here, the trail follows the crest south to Inspiration Point and Pass, the border of the Bob Marshall Wilderness. Roads, visible on Forest Service maps, also lead to trails that eventually reach this divide route. Inspiration Pass is a major northerly route into the northern sectors of the Bob Marshall Wilderness. From Inspiration Point south, the range becomes more spectacular and much wilder. The canyons become very steep and restricted with raging torrents of water flowing through them in the spring. Just south of Inspiration Pass, 9,289-foot Swan Peak, one of the major sentinels of the Swan Range, rises. This is one of the few summits in the Bob Marshall country holding active glaciers. These rivers of ice, found along the east and north sides of the peak, are kept alive by very heavy winter snows. Nestled far below Swan Peak is Sunburst Lake, a high cirque treasure.

South of Swan Peak, Lion Creek Pass offers another important route into the Bob by way of Palisades and Little Salmon creeks. The route up the Swan-face side goes through some beautiful stands of giant cedars. Farther down range, Smith Creek Pass is another course to the Swan summits and eventually into the South Fork country. The trail joins up with the one coming over Lions Creek Pass to Little Salmon Creek.

Top of Prairie Reef - 1945. U.S. FOREST SERVICE

Top: The Rocky Mountain Front. LARRY MAYER
Bottom: North of Birch Creek. RICK AND SUSIE GRAETZ

57

Top: Sunset on the Rocky Mountain Front. RICK AND SUSIE GRAETZ
Bottom: First light sets Sawtooth Reef on fire. RICK AND SUSIE GRAETZ

Top: The overthrust belt in the Rocky Mountain Front. RICK AND SUSIE GRAETZ
Bottom: The Heart Butte area on the Northern Front. RICK AND SUSIE GRAETZ

Top: Hazel Ridge, named after legendary Paul Hazel, from Beartop Mountain.   RICK AND SUSIE GRAETZ
Bottom: Spring hits the Rocky Mountain Front.   RICK AND SUSIE GRAETZ

The South Fork of the Teton and Rocky Mountain Peak.   RICK AND SUSIES GRAETZ

Top: One of the sentinels of the Rocky Mountain Front – Ear Mountain.   RICK AND SUSIE GRAETZ
Bottom: Looking into the Bob Marshall from the north slopes above Gibson Lake.   RICK AND SUSIE GRAETZ

Top: Near Heart Butte and Feather Woman mountains on the Rocky Mountain Front.   RICK AND SUSIE GRAETZ
Bottom: Looking toward the Badger – Two Medicine area on the Rocky Mountain Front.   RICK AND SUSIE GRAETZ

63

The Rocky Mountain Front from above the Choteau Mountain area.   RICK AND SUSIE GRAETZ.

Top: Bighorn Peak and the Continental Divide.   BILL CUNNINGHAM
Bottom: Hahn Peak and the North Wall.   RICK AND SUSIE GRAETZ

Spring wildflowers on the Front.   RICK AND SUSIES GRAETZ

Top: Rocky Mountain Front seems to stretch out toward infinity.   RICK AND SUSIE GRAETZ
Bottom: Reefs of the Rocky Mountain Front from near Sullivan Hill.   RICK AND SUSIE GRAETZ

Top: Sawtooth Reef. RICK AND SUSIE GRAETZ
Bottom: The Blackleaf Canyon area. RICK AND SUSIE GRAETZ

Top: Max Baucus and Jamie Williams on top of Ear Mountain.   RICK AND SUSIE GRAETZ
Bottom: Looking down Pot Shot Creek.   BILL CUNNINGHAM

From the top of Rocky Mountain Peak looking down the South Fork of the Teton toward the Rocky Mountain Front. RICK AND SUSIES GRAETZ

Top: Winter on the North Fork of the Teton River.   RICK AND SUSIE GRAETZ
*Bottom: The beginnings of the South Fork of the Teton on the trail to
Headquarters Pass.*   RICK AND SUSIE GRAETZ

Crow Peak and the Carmichael Basin in the Scapegoat Country.. U.S. FOREST SERVICE PHOTO

Just west of Condon, the second highest pinnacle in the Bob Marshall country, 9,356-foot Holland Peak, reaches to the clouds. Considered by many to be the most spectacular summit in the Swan Range, it sits amidst a jumble of other towering mountains, and is characterized by two huge waterfalls emanating from the Upper and Lower Rumble Creek lakes just below its west face. The east side of this massif, features several active glaciers. Forest Service maps show more glaciers than actually exist. For instance, those supposed to be in Albino Basin, just to the north of Holland Peak, are probably no more than persistent snowfields that disappear some years.

Holland Peak, like many others along the Swan Range, requires quite a physical effort to gain the top. The relief here ranges upwards of 5,500 feet, and much of it is darned vertical. South of Holland Peak, and extending for many miles, are beautiful basins holding high cirque lakes. Routes leading in to the Bob go through some of these areas. Holland Lake is a starting point for many of the trails, as well as two of the major routes into the Bob Marshall country from the west. Sitting astride, or just below, the Divide are bodies of water such as the Terrace Lakes, Woodward Lake, the Necklace Lakes, Pendant Lakes, Upper Holland Lake, Lick Lake, Koessler Lake, Doctor Lake and George Lake, to name a few. To the people of the Swan Valley this is the best country in Montana .

The trails out of Holland Lake, favorites of horse packers, are steep and get one into the backcountry in a hurry. The two major routes are over Gordon Pass from Upper Holland Lake and down Gordon Creek into the South Fork of the Flathead, or via the Pendant or Necklace lakes to Big Salmon Creek and Big Salmon Lake. The distances from Holland Lake into the deep backcountry are great and most people would rather use horses. We have hiked across the Bob Marshall and prefer to take it from east to west, coming out at Holland Lake.

From the Seeley Lake area, Pyramid Pass offers access to the upper reaches of the South Fork of the Flathead drainage. Trails from here lead to Youngs Creek. Other less-used passes are in the vicinity of Monture Mountain. Youngs Pass is another popular trail and also leads to Youngs Creek. Hahn Creek Pass, out of the Monture Creek country on the southern end of the range in the Blackfoot Valley, is another well-used horse route into the upper stretches of the South Fork country.

Because of the terrain, the eastern flanks of the Bob Marshall country offer more roaded access to the wilderness boundary than does the Swan side. However, there is ample access in the lower reaches of the Swan Valley to enable motorized vehicle enthusiasts to get a closer look at some of the steep slopes and high peaks of the Swan Range. There are loop logging roads off of the Swan highway that rise to high ridge lines and open to excellent views. The Swan Range, then, just like the Rocky Mountain Front, offers something for everyone.

North Fork of Birch Creek Country.

WEATHER
by Rick and Susie Graetz

The vastness and diversity of the Bob Marshall country dictates varied and unpredictable weather. One thing is for certain, the Bob experiences it all ... 100 degrees above zero to 60 degrees below, drought to floods, bottomless snow to raging blizzards, and from deafening winds to sweet silence.

The Continental Divide serves as a sky-scraping barrier that robs moisture from many of the storm systems crossing this wilderness country; hence, most of the precipitation falls on the Divide and the Swan Crest to its west. The Swan Range, itself a formidable wall, takes so much precipitation that there are small glaciers surviving on the north sides of several peaks. This phenomenon is evidenced by the denser vegetation cover on the west side; the closer to prairie country and the Rocky Mountain Front, the sparser the growth. Strong winds on the east side take moisture from the soil, further hindering growth.

It is possible to watch a storm in progress along the Chinese Wall from just a few miles to the east with no threat of getting wet. The stronger front systems minimize the mountain obstacles and can spread their moisture on both sides of the Divide. These stronger systems have enough power and moisture in them to avoid the down-draft, drying-out effect as the moist air crosses the Divide. The storms that don't make it over places like Scapegoat and the Chinese Wall simply dry out as the air that has just risen to cross the barrier starts warming on its descent to the east side of the mountains.

In places like the North Fork of Birch Creek or the Teton Canyons, on the eastern fringes of the Bob, it's interesting to watch east-flowing clouds grow smaller and disappear.

Thunderstorms of late spring and summer are usually spawned along the Divide and the higher ranges. The air rises rapidly as it heats, creating intense storms that move anywhere regardless of terrain. That is they are not part of weather systems that follow specific directions east to west, etc.

As a whole, the greatest amount of precipitation in the Bob comes in the spring, especially May and June; although in the higher peaks, the distribution throughout most of the year is more even.

Snow is also heaviest in the spring months; however, east of the Divide, especially along the Rocky Mountain Front, some of the deepest snowfall usually occurs during the cold months of December, January and February. The process that brings these storms to the Rocky Mountain Front region is known as up-sloping. Systems coming from the southeast carry warm, moist Gulf of Mexico air that collides with the frigid arctic air sitting along the Front. Precipitation becomes quite intense owing to the abrupt uplifting of air. It is possible for these storms to travel into the Bob, because the mountains to the west create more uplifting; however, the farther west, the lighter the snow.

This same procedure is often responsible for the drenching rainstorms or early fall snows that the Bob Marshall east of the Divide often experiences. The southeast systems can cause the northerly winds that trail them to pull cold air from the north, further intensifying and deepening the cold air mass.

The Rocky Mountain Front is known for its chinook winds, or snow-eaters as the Indians called them. When they occur, the temperature may rise from 30 degrees below zero to 30 degrees above within a couple of hours or less. There have been reports of a 26-degree rise in 45 seconds, and 43 degrees in 15 minutes.

The chinooks result from a steady, warm and moist westerly or southwesterly flow of air across Montana. This pattern also shows a high-pressure system to the south of the state over Nevada and Utah, and a low-pressure system to the north in Canada. As the moisture-laden winds begin to rise to cross the mountains of the Bob, they release their precipitation, usually in the form of heavy wet snow, on the uphill side. As they come rapidly down the mountain front, they become warmer and drier. At times their approach is heralded by a freight-train-like sound through the down-slope canyons.

The country east of the Chinese Wall also witnesses another extreme — that of severe cold, a result of arctic outbreaks. If the arctic air is deep enough, and comes on strong north winds, the cold air spills over to the valleys west of the Divide, putting the entire wilderness complex in a dome of very cold air. Temperatures may reach 40 to 60 degrees below zero. The record low temperature for the contiguous 48 states was set on the southern edge of the Bob Marshall country at Rogers Pass when the mercury dipped to 70 degrees below zero on January 20, 1954. Actually it was probably colder, the thermometer's minimum mark was minus 70 and that reading was observed at 2:00 a.m. — the coldest temperature usually occurs just before sunrise.

Whereas chinooks transpire in winter when the storm track moves into Canada, the arctic air is brought down by the storm trails moving far to the south of Montana. While the chinook winds cause rapid warming along the

Rocky Mountain Front, the cold northern air has the opposite effect. At Browning, just east of the Front, the temperature once plummeted from a 44 degrees above zero to 56 degrees below zero in 24 hours.

In describing the general weather pattern of the Bob Marshall it is necessary to keep in mind that in some years there can be great fluctuations.

Summers are warm and dry with occasional thunderstorms. West of the Divide the humidity is a bit higher and their storms may occur with greater frequency. East of the Divide the air is more arid and often the temperatures are higher, with 90 to 100 degrees not uncommon. As summer turns to fall, some of the greatest temperature variations occur. Often it maybe 40 degrees warmer in the afternoon than at first light. At this time of the year the sun is up long enough to heat the day and because the nights are longer, radiation cooling takes place.

Most likely, in early September a week or two of storminess prevails; in the higher elevations the snow pack begins to accumulate right after Labor Day. After this interlude of unsettled weather, usually, a big high-pressure ridge builds over the west and the Bob Marshall country enjoys clear, dry air with warm days and crisp nights. By November, the snow pack is beginning to build in the valleys.

As winter settles in, the tempests, especially west of the Divide, increase and the colder air begins filling the lower elevations. November, December and January are stormy months in the Bob. East of the Divide it is often very cold. When this arctic air from the east seeps through the canyons and over the mountains to the west side of the Divide, fierce ground blizzards transpire as northerly winds are pushing the cold air into this section of the wilderness. Below zero readings and a low wind chill are common. In February and early March, longer periods of clear, cold weather seem to be more prevalent. From late March through June, this country receives much of its annual precipitation. Snow is usually the dominant form of precipitation well into May, and then the heavier rains come.

The annual snow pack in winter and spring is quite variable; individual seasons can have as little as 50 percent of average to as high as 170 percent of the norm. Since about 70 percent of the spring and summer stream flow comes from winter snow, its accumulation has a marked effect on runoff.

In late April, the lower elevations and south facing slopes begin to lose their snow cover, and the streams start to rise slowly. By mid-May, the lower areas are usually bare, and all areas with snow cover are showing considerable melting, swelling the streams to their maximum flows. As the snowline recedes, streams begin to drop and clear. However, the snow remains in the higher elevations into July, aiding the water supply of the stream systems. There are periods of clear skies during the spring and some years can be quite dry, but for the most part the weather is very unsettled this time of the year as the warming air holds more moisture.

Snow Surveys

Because of its size, the Bob Marshall eco-system is very important to the overall water supply of much of Montana. It is for this reason that there are about 30 snow courses throughout the wilderness and surrounding areas. These courses are measured from three to seven times each year, and the data gathered is used primarily for forecasting potential runoff during the spring and early summer.

Ray Mills now retired from the Rocky Mountain Ranger District, out of Choteau, covering almost all of the Bob Marshall country east of the Divide, had measured the snow-course sites in these areas from 1968 until recently. He primarily covered the courses in the Sun River drainage. They are located at Cabin Creek, Wrong Creek, Wrong Ridge and Goat Mountain. The route he covered was about 76 miles and took six to eight days to complete, depending upon the snow conditions. As this is wilderness, travel was by snowshoes or skis, and he preferred to use snowshoes. He has seen the all-time high snow measurement in this area, as well as the all-time low. In 1972 Ray measured 94.4 inches of snow on March 1 at Wrong Ridge and 29 inches of water content. On March 1, 1981 at the same site, he measured only 33.2 inches of snow and 9.9 inches of water. Normal water content for March 1 is 18.3 inches and about 60 inches of snow.

Kraig Lang, now the wilderness ranger out of the Choteau station has taken over Mill's duties. He covers the same courses and prefers skis, taking four to six days to finish.

Using a two-inch diameter aluminum tube, the snow depth is recorded when the rim on the bottom comes in contact with the ground. The pipe with its snow core is carefully lifted out and then weighed. Subtracting the weight of the empty tube from the total gives the water content in inches. A graph of snow depth and water content shows the percent of water or density in the snow pack, which varies greatly from year to year and even from month to month. The course measurements in the Sun River country are taken three times a year.

The following is a chart showing the various snow courses in or near the Bob Marshall Wilderness and come from the Natural Resources Conservation Service and were supplied to us by Roy Kaiser, Water Supply Specialist out of Bozeman, Montana. The measurements shown were taken on April 1. The deeper snow readings are from sites west of the Divide. For instance, Camp Misery and Noisy Basin are in the Swan Range to the west of Hungry Horse Lake. Mt. Lockhart is at Teton Pass ski area in the Rocky Mountain Front country.

The actual average snowfall in the Bob Marshall Wilderness, in the higher elevations, ranges from 300 to 500 inches a year. Some sites get more and others get quite a bit less.

SNOTEL means Snow Pack Telemetry and is an automated system that sends data several times a day. Blanks in the columns means no information was available until recently.

Snow Courses in/near Bob Marshall Wilderness

Site Name	Elevation Feet	Start of Record	April 1 Average Depth Inches	Max Measured Depth Inches	Year of Max Depth	1971-2000 Average Apr 1 SWE Inches
Badger Pass SNOTEL	6900	1989				35.3
Big Creek	6750	1941	109	155	1972	43.7
Blue Lake	5900	1969	62	104	1972	23.7
Cabin Creek	5200	1949	21	41	1954	5.4
Camp Misery	6400	1962	120	172	1974	49.3
Copper Bottom SNOTEL	5200	1991				11.0
Copper Camp SNOTEL	6950	1983				32.4
Copper Creek	5700	1962	38	79	1972	13.3
Coyote Hill	4200	1947	27	54	1997	8.7
Desert Mountain	5600	1937	44	70	1950	14.7
Emery Creek SNOTEL	4350	1990				15.3
Fatty Creek	5500	1962	67	114	1997	24.3
Five Bull	5700	1948	20	46	1971	5.5
Freight Creek	6000	1948	45	81	1972	14.8
Goat Mountain	7000	1934	34	56	1954 & 1956	9.7
Gunsight Lake	6300	1964	99	140	1972	39.3
Holbrook	4530	1951	25	58	1978	8.2
Marias Pass	5250	1934	49	94	1954	16.8
Mount Lockhart SNOTEL	6400	1989				21.1
Noisy Basin SNOTEL	6040	1990				40.9
North Fork Jocko SNOTEL	6330	1990				45.3
Spotted Bear Mountain	7000	1948	41	72	1948	14.1
Trinkus Lake	6100	1949	106	164	1997	42.0
Twin Creeks	3580	1951	27	64	1972	9.6
Upper Holland Lake	6200	1948	92	135	1971	34.6
Waldron SNOTEL	5600	1990				10.8
Wrong Creek	5700	1949	40	73	1954 & 1972	12.3
Wrong Ridge	6800	1949	55	94	1972	18.0

WILDLIFE
by Bob Cooney

I have had the good fortune of being closely associated with the wildlife of the Bob Marshall since the early 1930s. For several years with the Forest Service, I gathered information on the elk herds and other game animals of that area, and spent nearly 30 years with the Montana Fish and Game Department in game management. Throughout that time, the department put an emphasis on wilderness wildlife. Since retirement, I've made many hiking and horseback trips to the backcountry.

The material in this chapter has been gained through personal observations over many years and from the findings of others especially knowledgeable of the area. The presentation is not formal. I have thought of it much as though we were visiting around a campfire back in those remote mountains.

Mammals

Since elk have played such an important role in the wildlife picture of the entire area, it might be well to begin with them.

This is truly elk country. There are several major herds identified by their home ranges. These are the Sun, the South Fork of the Flathead, and the Middle Fork of the Flathead rivers' herds. Another fairly large group summers in the upper North Fork of the Blackfoot River drainage. Other scattered bands are found around the edge of this vast area.

Because they are wild and shy, you may not see many elk, but evidence of their presence is frequent.

A network of elk trails crisscrosses the area. Some lead to favorite feeding and resting places, others to heavily frequented natural licks. Well-worn migration trails traverse high divides. Heavily scarred little pines indicate the early fall activity of bull elk in cleaning and polishing their antlers for the rutting season. Small mud wallows also can be found in these same areas as further evidence of bulls' activities in the fall.

Winter ranges are the most critical to the life of the elk. It is possible to recognize these important places even during summer visits. Favored shrubs, such as willows, often show the results of heavy browsing. Nearby, lodge pole pine thickets bear evidence of high-lining where wintering elk had resorted to eating the needles as high as they could reach when more favored food was not available. Scars appear on aspen boles where elk have scraped off bits of bark as winter food. And the ever-present, weather-resistant compact droppings indicate elk have wintered there.

Newborn calves enhance the loveliness of springtime in these mountains. The cows select calving grounds with care. Usually, they are along the migration routes from winter to higher summer ranges. They must be below the receding snow line of late May and early June. In such places, lush plant growth assures a plentiful milk supply.

The newly born spotted calves are difficult to see lying motionless among low, shrubby plants, often along the edge of an aspen grove. Of course the cows are very protective; they seem to have little difficulty in chasing away coyotes, but bears occasionally present a more serious problem. In such cases a number of cows will sometimes join together in an attempt to discourage the intruder.

With the coming of summer, cows and calves move up toward the heads of drainages to high, partially wooded basins. Strong, proficient swimmers, they have no trouble fording the swollen, fast-moving streams. If they are disturbed, the anxious calling of both the cows and calves creates a compelling sound that aids in keeping them together as they move through the forest.

The bulls generally spend the summers in somewhat the same areas, but stay pretty much by themselves. While the cows raise the calves, the male's typically demanding days are spent feeding, resting and growing new antlers.

Elk tend to move to slightly lower areas with the coming of early fall and the rutting season. This is a time of great activity among the bulls. They use large amounts of energy in attempting to collect and hold groups of cows and calves — called harems — and warding off the competition. There seems to be more bluffing and sparring than actual fighting, but the bulls do get serious at times. The thrilling, high-pitched bugling of the males rings out across wooded canyons, even throughout the nights.

Bob Marshall elk herds have interesting histories. All have developed from small native groups that were back in these mountains around the turn of the century.

The Sun River Game Preserve established by the Montana Legislature in 1912 is an outgrowth of early concern for the preservation and development of elk. This area of approximately 200,000 acres lies west from the North and South Forks of the Sun River to the Continental Divide. It is presently looked upon with mixed feelings. Some maintain that, although it may have had beneficial effects on the early growth of the elk herd, it now presents problems in regard to gaining better elk distribution and a more orderly harvest. Others feel it still possesses value as a wildlife sanctuary.

In its development, the Sun River elk herd faced especially difficult problems. Early on, they had to compete with large numbers of cattle well back into the forest. In spite of this, there was a steady increase among the herd. By the mid-'20s, numbers had risen to a point where elk began to drift out onto private lands along the foothills during the winter months.

Even with the removal of all cattle from the upper Sun River ranges in the early '30s, elk continued to drift to private lands outside the mountains. It became such a problem that the Department of Fish and Game assigned a pioneer warden, the late Bruce Neal, to devise ways of turning the elk back into the deep-snow country of the forest and holding them there. He conducted this difficult task for some 17 winters. I had a first-hand look at the work in helping Bruce with the herding a number of times. Sportsmen and ranchers also aided in this difficult task.

Occasionally, about a thousand elk were moved at a time. They were pressed back along steep and snow-packed migration trails. Even with all this effort, the program was not a solution. The underlying problem remained a lack of winter range to support this major herd.

Other related problems were becoming increasingly evident. These large bands of elk being held back in the mountains were then competing seriously with bighorn sheep. Heavy winter losses took place among the bighorns, especially along the Sun River Canyon where elk were overusing additional bits of available winter range above the canyon on both forks of the river.

The future for the Sun River elk herd looked very bleak by the mid-'40s. It seemed inevitable that elk numbers would have to be drastically reduced, probably to a point where they would lose identity as a nationally recognized herd.

A break came in 1948. Two large adjoining ranch holdings in the foothills became available for purchase. It was the very grass and rolling timberlands the elk had been trying to reach during all those winters. This beautiful foothill range, just south of the Sun River and east of the massive Sawtooth Mountain, west of Augusta, was ideal to meet the winter needs of the long beleaguered herd. As wonderful as it appeared for the elk, the Fish and Game Department found it would be impossible to act fast enough to meet the very short deadline specified by the sellers. And out-of-state money was ready to make the purchase.

It looked as though this chance of a lifetime for the Sun River elk herd was slipping away. At that critical point, Tom Messelt, a sportsman from Great Falls, and Carl Malone, a rancher from Choteau, got together and made the necessary down payments. They held the land until the acquisition process by the State could be completed.

Soon after the State Fish and Game Department acquired the range, the late Dr. Olaus Murie, an internationally recognized wildlife authority, called it one of the very finest winter elk ranges on the continent, visited it. The 20,000-acre range was quickly made ready for use by elk, and they lost no time in reaching it.

Now, the elk traveled quickly through the bighorn sheep winter range along the Sun River Canyon. The bighorns, after years of competition with the elk, began a steady increase in numbers. The long-standing winter problem of elk on private lands along the foothills also greatly improved. Bruce Neal, who for all those years had to push the elk that he loved back into the deep snow, was made the first manager of the game range. It is easy to imagine that for him it was a dream comes true.

Work on the game ranges is continuous. Frequent horseback and snowshoe patrols are conducted and occasionally a helicopter makes passes during winter months to maneuver outlying groups of elk onto the range. Many miles of specially designed boundary fence, consisting of jacks and barbed wire with a jumping rail along the top, had to be constructed. The rail was necessary so elk could gauge their jumps in moving on and off the range. It is stockproof, but the elk have no problem jumping it.

In the summer and fall there is fire patrol as a grassfire could be disastrous to the winter forage supply for the elk. The manager is available for field trips over the range by school groups and others from surrounding communities. He also helps with the wildlife work being conducted on the range and in the wilderness. Recreational visitors drop in throughout the year. In the winter, the manager can suggest the best views of the elk without disturbing them.

There have been short hunting seasons on the range in the fall before major numbers of migrating elk leave. Some tend to linger on the winter range year-round; and a fall harvest of these animals ensures as much grass as possible will be available for the critical period ahead.

In more recent years, the Montana Department of Fish, Wildlife and Parks and The Nature Conservancy have acquired additional winter range areas north of the Sun River. These important foothill and swamplands lie north and south of the Teton Canyon, along the Rocky Mountain Front. They provide important winter foraging areas for elk and deer as well as highly valuable habitat for grizzly bears.

The Sun River elk herd, which has gone through such difficult times, faces a bright future unless seriously disrupted by oil and gas exploration and development on the vital winter ranges or along the elk's major migration routes. The South and Middle Forks of the Flathead elk herds have been quite similar in their development. From the standpoint of the elk, both benefited from extensive forest fires that swept through these mountain areas in the early part of this century. Willow, serviceberry, mountain maple and other browse (brushy plants) soon sprung up throughout the burned areas. As these plants stood up well in the snow, they became a very important part of the winter food supply for steadily increasing numbers of elk.

The situation began to change as the years went by. Slower growing lodgepole pine appeared in dense stands throughout these old burns. The pines gradually crowded and shaded out many of the browse plants reducing the amount of winter forage available. Heavy elk population losses have been experienced, particularly during severe winters.

A recent Forest Service policy may allow wild fire to again assume something of its historic role in plant succession, therefore allowing an increase in forage plants.

Mule and white-tailed deer frequent many areas in the Bob Marshall country. The white-tails are often found in timber and brushy meadows along stream and river bottoms, the mule deer prefer the rougher terrain. Both often make lengthy treks to and from their winter ranges. Recent findings have indicated a portion of the mule deer that winter along the eastern edge of the Rocky Mountain Front drift long distances to the west into the very heart of the Bob to spend the summers.

Both species prefer leaves, buds and twigs of browse plants and even juniper and fir needles for winter feed. At least on the eastern side of the Continental Divide, their choice of diet differs considerably from the grass so favored by elk and bighorn sheep.

The unique, stiff-legged, bouncing pace of running mule deer makes them look as though they are going up and down about as much as forward, but this method of travel is well adapted to the rocky, rough country where they live. Sometimes, this gait has its disadvantages. For example along the Sun River Canyon in the winter, coyotes occasionally chase mule deer out onto the ice of Gibson Lake. Tracks show that the deer, so sure footed on rough hillsides, are badly handicapped when running on ice.

Deer often come into summer camps in the daylight in the mountains. They seem salt hungry and will lick or chew anything salty. Horseback riders have found it best to hang up their gear or cover it with canvas. A friend in camp up near the Continental Divide had placed his saddle near his tent for the night. At daylight he was startled to see his bridle go scooting by the open tent flap. He looked out and was just in time to see a mule deer doe departing across the meadow with one of the reins in her mouth.

Bighorn sheep are found for the most part on the eastern side of the Bob Marshall country. They often move some distance from high summer ranges to winter along south facing rocky slopes that are interspersed with patches of grass.

The sheep have gone through some difficult times. From the '20s up to the purchase of the elk winter range in the foothills in 1948, losses continued periodically. With the elk problem taken care of, the bighorns have increased until they are now one of the finest groups of this relatively rare animal in the United States. Animals captured in the Sun River Canyon area have started a number of newly developing herds of bighorns in other parts of Montana.

Big rams with their massive curled horns spend much of their time apart from the ewes, lambs and young rams. Many drift well north along the high crest of the Rocky Mountain Front Range. Almost overnight they appear among the ewes with the onset of the mating season in the late fall. This is an exciting time to watch the struggles for supremacy among the rams and to hear the sharp crack of horns slamming together in bouts between these powerful and blocky-built combatants. With the end of the mating season many of the rams appear to patch up their differences as they move off in small groups.

Mountain goats are a breed apart. Their wide range of food selection, heavy cold-resistant coats and superb mountaineering ability make it possible for them to live year round in a soaring, harsh environment. They are found singly or in small, scattered bands along the mountain crests of much of the Bob Marshall Wilderness.

Because of the goats' apparent dislike of becoming rain soaked, their home ranges are often in convenient proximity to overhanging cliff faces or shallow caves. Only if you are lucky or persistent will you catch a glimpse of moving white specks threading their way along narrow ledges on high precipitous cliffs.

The goats' dagger-sharp, curving horns are truly formidable weapons. A lightning-fast thrust of the head can inflict destructive damage. It is no wonder they have gained the respect of even the larger predators that occasionally frequent their alpine homeland.

The kids, born early June, stay close to their mothers, but can soon perform surprising feats of rock climbing. If a golden eagle should soar near, the little fellows frequently take a position directly beneath their mothers, and those who study the goat believe that eagles do not present a very serious threat to the kids. Mountain goats have been captured in several places in the Bob and successfully transplanted into new ranges.

As far as we know, moose have not been abundant in the Bob Marshall area. These big fellows are presently found rather thinly scattered in willow thickets and adjoining timberlands along the Middle Fork of the Flathead and its side drainages. They are widely dispersed in the lower South Fork of the Flathead drainage and farther upriver in the Youngs Creek-Danaher area. Moose occasionally are seen in the Gates Park region along the North Fork of the Sun River on the east side of the Divide. Their long legs make it possible for them to winter in areas where snow becomes quite deep.

The grizzly bear or silvertip is surely the animal that best typifies the true wild character of the wilderness. Just to see its great claw-tipped tracks in some muddy place along a mountain trail is an unforgettable thrill. That they are here at all is due to the retention of a few large undisturbed mountain strongholds where these huge, but relatively reticent, animals can survive. Human activities have eliminated them from almost all of their former range throughout the west south of the Canadian border. Glacier Park and adjoining areas and the Bob Marshall Wilderness country make up the very core of the vital Northern Continental Divide Grizzly Range. All of the requirements of this big bear are found here, especially a spacious, generally undisturbed environment.

Grizzlies have been classified as omnivorous, subsisting on a wide variety of food material, both plant and animal. They usually leave their winter dens in late March or early April. Some of the females would have given birth to cubs in their dens during mid-winter. They then move to lower elevations to feed upon grasses and forbs (weed-like plants) and seek out the remains of any animals that died during the winter. With the coming of summer, many of the bears work their way to higher elevations where they dig and consume tubers, fleshy roots and bulbs. They are well equipped with their long claws for this type of foraging. In their constant search for food, many rocks are turned over and stumps and rotten logs torn apart to obtain insects and larvae. Later in the summer, they usually turn their attention to ripening berries — with huckleberries the most favored. Where whitebark pine stands are available, at about 6,000 feet and above, the grizzlies search for nuts in the early fall. They often dig out squirrel caches to obtain this rich source of food.

Fieldwork by the internationally recognized Craighead brothers and others has documented that the big bears often have their winter dens dug and ready for occupancy by mid-fall. However, they apparently wait to go into them until a heavy snowstorm is in progress, perhaps in late November or early December. In that way, they leave no telltale tracks leading to their dens.

The future of the grizzly is troubled and it has been classified as a threatened wildlife species. This assures special consideration to the bear and to the critical wilderness habitat upon which its survival depends. During the Montana legislative session of 1983, the grizzly was designated the Montana State Animal.

The black bear, with its several color phases of brown, has somehow managed to avoid the threats to its existence that have plagued its big cousin, the grizzly. Found roaming in fair numbers throughout much of the Bob Marshall area, its home range seems often to include areas a bit lower in elevation than the grizzly. The black bear's food consists of a wide variety of plant and animal materials. Because it has adjusted fairly well to man's activities, its future is not as closely tied to the preservation of wilderness as has been so clearly demonstrated with the grizzly.

Classified as an endangered species, the gray wolf ekes out a precarious existence here, as an occasional visitor from Canada. The Glacier Park area and Bob Marshall Wilderness is a corridor of relatively undisturbed mountains serving as a link with the wolf populations in Canada to the north. A glimpse of a wolf, or even the faint sound of one howl, back in some remote place is a tremendous thrill. I know, because I heard one once, a long time ago up near the headwaters of the North Fork of the Sun River.

Coyotes and their tracks, as well as their droppings here and there along mountain trails, tell us these adaptable yet wary animals are very much a part of the wilderness. To be awakened with the first light of morning by their wild cries in the distance seems an especially fitting way to start the day. Their choice of food is varied. Mice, ground squirrels, birds, rabbits, and bits of carrion along with some plant material, are important items of their diet. If snow is deep and crusted, the deer break through, while the lighter coyotes can run on top, in this way, weak animals are sometimes taken.

Mountain lion or cougar, in Montana, has been classified as a game animal and is protected by quite restrictive regulations. Although a portion of the lion's requirements are satisfied by capturing smaller animals, deer and sometimes elk appear to make up the staple food of these big cats. They are found rather thinly dispersed throughout the Bob.

The Canada lynx is found in remote places throughout the Bob Marshall area. This stealthy animal is truly a creature of remote places. It lives out its life back in wooded areas where snowfall is heavy. Its large fur-covered paws allow it to travel swiftly over the snow. The snowshoe hare is believed to be its most important prey, and the lynx numbers are closely tied to the population cycles of the hare. The Canada lynx once was heavily trapped for its beautiful soft pelt it has been classified as a fur-bearing animal and carefully protected. As they are especially wary and do much of their hunting at night, it would be an exceptional stroke of luck to see one. Just to know they are there is pleasure enough for most lovers of wildlife.

The smaller bobcat prefers for the most part, the rough foothills and brushy canyon bottoms of the Rocky Mountain Front Range and other areas around the outer portion of the wilderness. There they search for cottontail rabbits and other small prey. They have been trapped quite heavily, but like the Canada lynx, have received increased protection since being placed on the fur-bearing animal list in the fur trade, the spots along the lower portions of their body might have placed them in demand among the spotted cats of the world for which there is increasing concern.

Beaver attracted the first explorer-trappers into this part of the west a century and a half ago. Gnawed aspen stumps, ponds, dams, lodges and food caches throughout river and stream bottoms are constant reminders of the presence of these energetic animals. The bark of quaking aspen and willows make up much of their diet in these mountains. Once all of the trees near their ponds have been cut down, the beavers become creatures of high risk. Now it is necessary to travel longer distances from the safety of water to obtain their food. Superb swimmers, they are rather slow on land where they are easy prey to a variety of the larger predators. Their ponds are keys to their survival. At some point, they find it essential to leave their homes and move on to construct new ones nearer an adequate food supply. Their lives are inseparably bound to water.

The beaver of the Bob Marshall and other mountain ranges have the unique ability to sometimes alter the landscape. Many meadows along mountain drainages may well have once been narrow and relatively steep streambeds. Meadowlands and gently meandering streams were created where beaver ponds had been made, abandoned and filled with silt then made again. It is quite possible that the beautiful meadows of the Danaher Basin, near the headwaters of the South Fork of the Flathead, had their origin through centuries of beaver activity.

River otter are the aquatic acrobats and clowns of the weasel family. Following their tracks in deep snow along one of the partially frozen rivers of the wilderness, reveals a series of running jumps and then a long slide … more jumps and another slide, continuing until they bring you to an opening in the ice littered with bits of fish, scales and crayfish scattered here and there. Now, you have found where otters, which can reach high speeds through the water as they search for elusive prey, swim and play.

Riverbanks of these same watercourses are homeland for the otter's small cousin, the mink. Wilderness fishermen are sometimes surprised to discover that the trout they momentarily left unattended along a bank, may well have disappeared by the time they returned. A hungry mink was quite possibly the culprit. As with all of the weasel tribe, they are voracious eaters, living on a variety of small animals, birds, crayfishes and fishes. In their search for food, this elegant member of the weasel family depends upon its ability as a good swimmer and climber.

The pine marten, sometimes called the American sable, is perfectly equipped for a life in mature timber stands. It prefers deep-snow country where its fur-covered paws enable it to rapidly bound over the soft fluffy stuff. Marten are able to rundown even the fleet snowshoe hares. And at a moment's notice, they are able to switch their hunting to the treetops, where pine squirrels top the menu.

A close relative of the pine marten, the fisher is considerably larger in size and darker in color. It too has been highly prized in the fur trade for the frosty sheen of its beautiful pelt. Apparently, the fisher had disappeared from the mountain ranges of Montana for many years. In the late 1950s, in a joint venture between the Department of Fish and Game and Forest Service, it was reintroduced from British Columbia. Sightings have been made within the Bob Marshall Wilderness along the heavily timbered west side of the South Fork of the Flathead.

Fishers are known for their speed through the treetops. As the marten can catch the pine squirrel, the fisher is said to be able to out-climb the marten. Its most unique prey is the plodding, but dangerously armed porcupine. The fisher has developed a lightning-like attack from the front to avoid the potentially lethal quills. Foresters have been interested in the reintroduction of the fisher as it might reduce damage to pine trees by holding down the numbers of the bark gnawing porcupines, thus restoring a historic balance.

Badgers are sometimes seen along the more open portions of the inter-mountain valleys of the Bob Marshall area, where they do a great deal of digging in search of ground squirrels and other rodents.

The wolverine must be the most striking of the weasel tribe. This legendary animal is unexcelled in strength by any creature its size. Somewhat bear-like in shape and weighing about 40 pounds, it was thought the wolverine was gone from much of its historic range in Montana. Some time ago, they began to reappear along the Continental Divide corridor out of Canada, through the Glacier Park area and down into the Bob Marshall Wilderness country. These mostly solitary animals travel great distances in their constant search for food. It has been especially pleasing to observe tracks of the wolverine on recent winter trips into the Bob. Even though they are back, they are seldom seen.

The weasel or ermine is sometimes seen darting here and there in the wilderness. This veritable streak of brown becomes snow white except for its black tipped tail during the winter months. Mice and other small prey make up the food supply of this curious and agile little predator.

The red or pine squirrel is a good example of the area's many non-game species. They act like self-appointed sentinels. Their boisterous chattering often follows as we move through these otherwise quiet woods. There is a love-hate relationship between these small squirrels and the immense grizzlies. The squirrels find great pleasure in storing away caches of nuts among the stands of whitebark pines. Digging out the nuts and feasting on them must be a great discovery for the big bear, but it can seriously deplete the squirrel's winter food supply.

Columbia ground squirrels and their burrows are often evident in the Bob Marshall. Seen throughout open grassy parks and meadowlands on both sides of the Continental Divide, the plump little fellows are constantly on alert, as many of the meat-eating birds and animals prey on them. Before you see them, you will hear their chirping sound used as a warning signal.

Evidences of a small, secretive rodent are often found throughout mountain meadows of the Bob Marshall Wilderness in the form of mounds of earth freshly pushed up from an elaborate system of subterranean tunnels. The seldom-seen animal is the northern pocket gopher. They are well equipped for their underground existence. External cheek pouches are used to transport food throughout their tunnels. These small rodents have especially well developed forearms with long sharp claws. These and their strong gnawing teeth make them ideally prepared for a lifetime of prodigious digging. Underground plant parts such as roots and bulbs are their primary food. They are active the year round. With the melting of the snow, serpentine patterns of dirt on the surface of the ground are unique reminders of their winter activities.

Although the slow moving porcupines are not seen very often, evidence of their feeding is obvious among many of the pine stands. They chew off patches of bark, especially during the wintertime. Also, the wily red fox is sometimes seen in these mountains.

The hoary or whistling marmot is well adapted to its remote homeland among rockslides and alpine meadows. It is sometimes seen and heard on the talus slopes along the base of the Chinese Wall and other high rocky areas of the Bob Marshall Wilderness country. Their piercing whistles carry for long distances. It must serve as a very effective warning of golden eagles that glide into view along the precipitous cliffs above them. Their burrows are ordinarily under a jumble of large rocks that protect them from most predators.

The delightful little pika is another resident of the rockslides at higher elevations. These active little fellows have short rounded ears, soft rabbit-like fur and no visible tail. They have a surprising number of names, among which are rock rabbit, little chief hare and haymaker. The last refers to their interesting habit of collecting various plants as a winter food supply. During the summer they dash out to the edge of the rockslides where they nip off green bits of grass and weeds. These are brought back to a convenient and sunny place among the rocks to cure. Dried plants from these small haystacks are relished as food throughout the long harsh winters. The hardy little pikas do not hibernate, but remain active in their snug homes beneath the rockslides and deep snow of the high country. Blending well with the rocks where they live, a chirping call is usually the first evidence of their presence, but like the ventriloquist, they do not appear to be where you heard the sound.

Birds

From the diminutive kinglet to the majestic golden eagle, winged creatures are a beautiful and vibrant part of the vast wildlife community of the Bob Marshall. Some spend only the summers, others are there throughout the year. Most, like the thrushes, are reticent, few, like the gray jays, are often quite tame.

Three of the grouse species that inhabit this wilderness are often seen. They are the blue, the ruffed and the spruce grouse. The fourth, found only by those who explore remote high places at timberline or above, is the rare white tailed ptarmigan, a beautiful small grouse, perhaps left over from glacial times. I still remember the first one I saw. It was early summer, on the crest of Prairie Reef, well above timberline. A pair of ptarmigan were picking away at some alpine plants nearby. Hastily, I grabbed a telephoto lens out of my backpack and began attaching the camera to the tripod. When I finally took my eyes off the equipment and glanced at the birds, they were nearly under the tripod, too near for the telephoto. These beautiful little grouse were in their mottled summer plumage, and blended with the alpine tundra surroundings. That winter, on a scramble up the Continental Divide at the head of Lick Creek on the North Fork of the Sun River, it was so icy I decided, against my better judgment, to leave my camera behind. From the top I was treated to a view of veritable sea of white peaks in all directions. And no camera! Then I began looking at a little object on a large windblown snow bank nearby. It turned out to be a ptarmigan, and this time, except for its dark eyes and bill, it was as white as the snow itself.

These beautiful little fellows are thinly scattered along the mountain crests of the Continental Divide and adjacent ranges in the Bob Marshall country. They are well adapted to the harsh environment in which they live year round. The long, hair-like feathers on their legs and feet enable them to walk easily on soft snow.

The spruce grouse or Franklin's grouse is often called fool hen because of its gentleness and apparent fearlessness around humans. These small birds and their chicks sometimes frequent trails in the deep woods where they may be seeking dusting opportunities. The mothers are very protective. I would occasionally make a squeaking sound like a chick. The little spruce hens would invariably fluff up and come toward me. I have often thought they wouldn't be that tame around a coyote or lynx. Like other grouse, their numbers fluctuate in a somewhat cyclic fashion through the years.

The larger blue grouse are quite wary. Nesting at rather low elevations along river and creek bottom areas throughout much of the Bob, they move their chicks up the slopes as the insects and berries develop. By early fall the grouse form flocks along the ridge tops where they frequently winter. During periods of storminess, they sometimes tunnel into soft snow banks to spend the nights.

The ruffed grouse are usually found in the vicinity of brushy canyon and river bottoms. Their drumming sound is a pleasing harbinger of the coming of spring.

Waterfowl are not especially abundant in this wilderness region. A female common merganser with her string of little ones is always fun to watch as they paddle their way up one of the mountain rivers. It is surprising how fast the young can follow their mother if disturbed. By using their feet and stubby little wings they scuttle quickly along the surface of the water.

The colorful, timid and uncommon harlequin ducks prefer fast moving waters along the upper reaches of the chilly mountain rivers on both sides of the Continental Divide. The male is a splendid sight with striking white markings on a slate blue and rusty reddish background. They are sea ducks that come in from coastal waters to nest and raise their young.

Mallards, golden eyes, teals and others are seen on small meandering streams, beaver ponds and mountain lakes. Common loons visit Big Salmon Lake. Their plaintive, wild cry is another of the lovely sounds of that remote area.

It is always a treat to hear the hooting of a great horned owl in the quiet of a wilderness night. Among other owls of interest living here are the pygmy, barred, saw-whet and now and then the rare great gray owl.

The loud cadence of the pileated woodpecker's pecking breaks the silence of the deep woods. Fairly rare and almost the size of a crow, it is assuredly a bird of special interest. Seeming to prefer old-growth forests with a scattering of dead trees for nest building and feeding, they excavate nesting cavities 18 inches deep and up to 8 inches in diameter with an entrance somewhat rectangular to triangular in shape. Preparing new nesting places each year, their old ones provide ideal homes for other birds and small tree-climbing animals.

The common raven is a very interesting and intelligent bird. Somehow, it always gives the impression of knowing everything that is going on. In the fall, when hunters are about and an elk is killed, the message gets around among the ravens that food is available and where. Their coarse croaking calls, interspersed with chuckling sounds and now and then a few musical notes, come about as close to bird conversation as we might ever hear.

The Steller's and gray jays are not only very different in color, but also in temperament. The dark blue Steller's with its erect saucy crest and raucous voice are surely among the noisiest birds. They seem to enjoy imitating the whistling call of the red-tailed hawk. They also seem quite suspicious of man and his activities.

The lifestyle of the mild-mannered, quiet gray jay is about as different as it could be from that of their cousin. It is not unusual that camp is hardly set up before one or more of these unassuming little fellows drifts in. Their muted, whispering call is much in character with these friendly birds that appear to like people.

The sight of the dipper, or water ouzel, is always a special treat. The lives of these slate colored small birds are inseparably linked with the fast flowing waters of mountain rivers and streams. It is fun to watch them dive into rushing water and disappear to search for food, propelling themselves through the water with their stubby muscular wings. Nests are made of bits of moss and grasses woven into a dome shaped structure. They are always found close to the water, occasionally protected by the curtain of a waterfall. The dipper has been called the only truly aquatic songbird.

Another pleasant surprise was to find gray-crowned rosy finches high along the mountaintops in the homeland of the ptarmigan and the mountain goat. Some of the other birds of the Bob Marshall that quickly come to mind are the thrushes, fly catchers, juncos, warblers, Clark's nutcrackers, kingfishers, sparrows, the flash of color that turns out to be the western tanager, the chickadees, nuthatches, as well as the diminutive kinglets. And surely we cannot forget the hummingbirds.

There is something very special about the sight of golden or mountain eagles soaring among the high peaks. They surely typify the feeling of freedom and spaciousness of these remote places. Close glimpses of these large birds are rare and memorable.

Fish

The Continental Divide separates the Bob Marshall Wilderness country into several large headwater drainage areas. Each is quite distinct in regard to the fish that are found there. All have had interesting histories.

The large Sun River drainage system flows through the wilderness on the east side of the Divide. There was a high waterfall on the Sun River at the lower end of the canyon outside the wilderness, but the diversion dam obliterated it. This falls may well have presented a historic barrier to the upriver movement of fishes. Early reports indicate there were few if any originally above that point. Numerous early plantings were made. Brook, cutthroat and rainbow trout were introduced. Cutthroats seem to have preferred headwater streams. Brook trout have done best in the slower more meandering streams and beaver ponds, as well as the West Fork of the Sun River. Rainbows are found most frequently in Gibson Lake and above, in the larger reaches of both the North and South Forks of the Sun River. Trout also have been planted in several small mountain lakes.

In the mountains the Teton River system is so cold and clear that it is not highly productive of fish foods. It supports a rather light population of rainbow and brook trout, but there are cutthroats in the headwaters.

Fish on the western side of the Continental Divide in the Bob Marshall country are predominantly native species. Much of the west side fishery seems to have been developed around an ancient rhythm of spawning runs from Flathead Lake up into distant headwaters. The two major fishes are the westslope cutthroat trout and the bull trout, often called the Dolly Varden. The mountain whitefish, although not involved in such long spawning runs as the others, are found in quite large numbers in the rivers of the area.

The original range of the westslope cutthroat trout has been drastically reduced through the years. As a result, the Montana Department of Fish, Wildlife and Parks has designated this interesting and increasingly rare trout a Fish of Special Concern. An important reason for its decline has been the alteration of its natural habitat outside the wilderness. The introduction of exotic fish into some of its more easily reached waters, also has seriously affected the cutthroat. In addition to competition for food and space, the fact that the cutthroat readily hybridizes with rainbow trout has tended to eliminate pure populations, so important to the maintenance of its genetic integrity. Because of its significance as a truly wild, native trout, coupled with its historical value, the cutthroat has been designated as the Montana State Fish.

Fine trout with bright red slash markings that have given it the cutthroat name, is sometimes spoken of locally as a *"flat"* or *"blue back."* In the early spring, mature west slope cutthroats migrate out of Flathead Lake up the Flathead River and its tributaries. They may travel some 120 miles to spawn in the headwaters of the Middle Fork of the Flathead, well back in the wilderness. Since Hungry Horse Dam was constructed on the South Fork of the Flathead in the early 1950s, the spawning runs from Flathead Lake have been blocked. In the Jewel Basin area, on the northwestern edge of the region, high mountain lakes are numerous. Cutthroat trout and a few rainbows are found in these small but beautiful bodies of water hidden away in lovely wooded surroundings. Big Salmon is the largest lake in the upper South Fork being some four miles in length and half a mile in width. Cutthroat and bull trout are found in this body of water. Several especially beautiful, glacier formed lakes lie along the west side of the Upper South Fork of the Flathead River drainage. For the most part, they contain cutthroat trout. It is believed that the cold, clear upper reaches of the South and Middle Forks of the Flathead River system in the Bob Marshall

Wilderness country form the last most secure stronghold of the west slope cutthroat trout. Its very survival may well depend upon these wild, unchanged rivers and streams.

Bull trout have shared these headwaters with the cutthroat and mountain whitefish for untold time. Until rather recently, this big fish was locally known as the Dolly Varden. It has been found that the name Dolly Varden should be applied to its close relative, a large sea-going fish living along the coast of Alaska and south to the state of Washington. Our bull trout spends its entire life in fresh water and is found from the state of Washington into Western Montana. In the late spring, mature bull trout, sometimes up to three feet in length and 10 to 20 pounds in weight, leave Flathead Lake on their long journey to their fall spawning areas near the headwaters of the Flathead River system. An important share of these spawning waters is within the Bob Marshall Wilderness. During their long up-river trek, these large trout feed upon mountain whitefish and any other aquatic creatures they can conveniently obtain. As fall approaches, their coloration becomes increasingly bright. They spawn in September and October, often in rather small side streams and then return to Flathead Lake.

The beautiful wilderness region lying south of Scapegoat Mountain presents an interesting fish population. Rainbow, cutthroat and bull trout are found in the North Fork of the Blackfoot River and its tributaries. The Landers Fork of the Blackfoot and its side streams, contain a wilderness fishery similar to that in the North Fork drainage. There are several beautiful mountain lakes in the area that contain cutthroat and rainbow trout. Arctic grayling are found in Heart Lake. On the east side, the scenic upper Dearborn River supports predominantly rainbow trout with cutthroat in the headwaters. It is truly a thrill to catch glimpses of large bull trout in deep, green pools of the Flathead and Blackfoot river systems. The fight of the cutthroat and the arching leap of the rainbow in the wild, unchanged waters of the Bob Marshall surely add much to the vast variety of lovely living things up there along the nation's high divide.

WILDLIFE MEMORIES by Bob Cooney

The Cycle of Life

It was January and the snow was piling up. My plan was to snowshoe up Indian Creek to White River Pass on the Continental Divide. After getting well up the drainage, I noticed a number of fresh coyote tracks. They came from several directions and converged at a point I couldn't yet see in the canyon below me. As I moved to where I could look down, three coyotes dashed away. A couple of ravens flew overhead making their wild croaking sounds. What I saw startled me. There In the canyon bottom in a jumble of deep snow was evidence of a real tragedy. Elk antlers and legs stuck up through the snow. It appeared that about six bull elk had perished. There was still evidence of how it had happened. Bits of a trail still showed where they had wallowed through deep snow on the north face of Indian Creek. High above where I was standing, their trail ended abruptly in the path of a snow avalanche.

I was there again, in early April, this time with my partner. We had come from the north, having spent several days snowshoeing along the base of the Chinese Wall. With the glittering ice and great snow cornices that had been formed out from the crest by winter winds, the Wall had been unforgettably beautiful. We reached the head of Indian Creek about mid-afternoon. Coyote tracks again told us we were getting close to where the bull elk had died in the snow avalanche. Ravens were still there, and something else had been added — big, sinister looking grizzly tracks. As we stood quietly looking over the area, we began to make out a pattern in the tracks, many were by the elk remains, the rest on a padded trail that led through the melting snow banks to a nearby outcropping of rocks and what looked to be a den. Mingled with the big tracks were some very small ones. We could make out that two little cubs had played on the snow banks during trips to and from the den. As far as we could tell, no tracks had left the area. We began to feel a little uneasy, standing on an open slope, apparently just across a small canyon from a mother grizzly and her cubs. Hoping they were taking a nap, we didn't linger.

On the way down the trail, I considered the events. Several bull elk bad been killed in the snow slide. Coyotes and ravens had feasted during the remainder of the winter. Now, with the first hint of spring, a grizzly mother emerged from the den with her cubs and found nearby, a welcome banquet. Death and life were playing out a sad, but hopeful, drama in that remote place far up on the eastern edge of the Continental Divide.

The Good Samaritin

On another cold mid-winter day, as the snow level deepened, most of the elk had drifted to lower elevations where forage was more available. A few were still wintering in the forest. Pawing through the snow for grass and weeds, as well as feeding on willow and aspen tips, some were even scraping off bits of aspen bark. I was on Elk Hill on the North Fork of the Sun River looking down through a grove of trees at an object I couldn't make out very well through the rapidly falling snow. As I approached, I could see it was a cow elk, whose head had become firmly lodged in the v-shaped gap between two closely growing aspen trees. She had apparently been reaching as far as she could to scrape off bark and must have slipped or the snow gave away. A slow death by starvation and freezing would have been inevitable, also, she was a perfect target for any passing coyote, and there were plenty in the area.

I took off my snowshoes and carefully climbed up through the aspen to get above her. Slowly, I wedged myself between the two trees that were holding her and pushed with all the strength I could muster until I felt them give a little. It must have been enough to relieve the pressure and she jerked her head free. The magnificent creature stood there for a moment and then trotted away. As I strapped on my snowshoes and continued on down the drainage, I will never forget the warm feeling that went through me. By a rare coincidence that winter day, I had been able to save the life of an elk, far back in the wilderness.

Screams in the Night

One of my first assignments with the Montana Fish and Game Department In the early 1940s was to carry out a field study on grizzly bears in the Bob Marshall Wilderness, so I am often asked if have had any close calls with grizzlies.

I had a partner, a big husky fellow by the name of Ray Gibler. He handled our little pack string as we moved through the mountains. Ray was great to be with, as the going never got too tough for him and he never complained about my camp cooking. One July we were camped in a little meadow up near the Continental Divide. It was a nice evening so we didn't put up our tent. As dusk settled in, we both noticed how nervous the horses were. The grass was good, but they didn't seem to settle down. Instead, they kept lifting their heads and glancing back into the deep surrounding timber. Neither of us mentioned it, but I am sure we were both thinking there must be a bear.

Some clouds drifted over soon after we turned, our little campfire was completely dead so it became extremely dark. Lying in our bedrolls about 20 feet apart, it must have been around midnight when I was awakened by a half muffled shout from Ray. I had understood that this was the time grizzly become very active and there was little question in my mind that one had him.

I can still recall my momentary reactions. Options flashed through my mind a mile a minute. One was to get down into my sleeping bag and lie perfectly still; two was to leap out and make a run for the trees. I had second thoughts about that as the trees were big old spruce with a lot of dead limbs and sharp needles, and I was sleeping in my BVD's. I like to feel option three would have been to try to figure out some way to help my partner, but all at once the heavy breathing and thrashing about stopped. Out of the black night came Ray's booming voice, *"Gosh darn, there's a mouse in my sleeping bag and it's bit the heck out of me."* Yes, I have toned down Ray's comments — otherwise it's a true story.

Bob Cooney contributed quite a bit towards the history as well as wildlife sections of this book. He is a native of the Helena and a graduate of the University of Montana School of Forestry and worked for many years with the U.S. Forest Service as a ranger and wildlife specialist including three years spent on elk study in the Bob Marshall Wilderness Country.

In 1940 he transferred to the Montana Fish and Game Department and for 25 years was in charge of the Game Management Division. He retired in 1971 and now lives in Helena.

BOB MARSHALL COUNTRY HISTORY NOTES
by Rick and Susie Graetz

One of our goals in assembling this book on the Bob Marshall country was to compile an anecdotal chronology of this vast wilderness complex.

The Bob Marshall country has always been wild. Hence, it has passed through time in relative peace and has escaped the kind of events that make news or are otherwise recorded. The very nature of the people who traveled through this mountainous land also dictated that little of its history would be written. The earlier days witnessed the passing of Indians and mountain men. There were a few attempts at homesteading, notably in the Danaher Basin region and in Gates Park. And, some prospectors no doubt searched in vain in the various gulches for minerals. In the late 1800s, horse parties — some private, others guided by outfitters — began visiting the landscape to take in its hunting, fishing and beauty. In many cases, these people blazed their own trails, but more often than not followed trails developed by game, the Indians and the first mountain men.

After the turn of the century, forest rangers of the newly created Forest Service began to patrol the backcountry. Very few of these people, and even fewer of those who preceded them, recorded much of what they experienced.

The Forest Service has made attempts to get some of these early-day rangers to record their memoirs on paper. Unfortunately, in the case of the Bob Marshall, very few accounts have survived. The most notable have been those of Charlie Shaw and Clyde Fickes. Much of what follows, is reprinted from Forest Service Publications and other historical documents. The balance comes from conversations with people who knew of early-day events including discussions with Allen and Mildred Chaffin and C. B. Rich, of Seeley Lake, Joe White of Choteau and Bob Cooney of Helena.

Charlie Shaw assembled a publication in the early 1960s for the Forest Service titled The Flathead Story. Shaw worked for more than 31 years with the Forest Service beginning in the 1920s. Thirty of the years were spent in the areas of the South and Middle Forks of the Flathead River, now in the Bob Marshall Wilderness. This publication covered much of the Flathead National Forest. The excerpts we used are about the Bob Marshall country only and were taken exactly as Shaw presented them in his fine publication.

Most of the history notes remain the same as we printed them in our first edition of Montana's Bob Marshall Country in 1985, hence the conversations recorded, and publications read were prior to 1985.

The Big Prairie Ranger Station taken in 1957. U.S. FOREST SERVICE PHOTO

Golden Eagle and young on the Rocky Mountain Front.   GUS WOLFE

Top: Band of Rocky Mountain Bighorn Sheep near Big George Gulch.   GUS WOLFE
Bottom: The Sun River Elk heard on the Rocky Mountain Front.   GUS WOLFE

Mountain lion. GUS WOLFE

Top: Young grizzly bear in the Bob Marshall.   BILL LANCASTER
Bottom: Moose.   GUS WOLFE

Top: Mountain goats on Scapegoat Mountain.   GUS WOLFE
Bottom: Bull elk in the North Fork of the Sun River Country.   BOB COONEY

Bald eagle in the Sun River Country. BILL LANCASTER

Top: From Ayers Peak looking toward the Jumbo-Wood Tick Complex.   GUS WOLFE
Bottom: Basin Creek in the South Fork of the Flathead.   GUS WOLFE

Top: From the top of Pentagon Mountain looking at Dean Lake and the North Wall.   RICK AND SUSIE GRAETZ
Bottom: The head of Red Shale Creek looking along the North Wall.   BOB COONEY

Top: Pat McGuffin and Kraig Lang above the North Fork of the Sun Valley.   RICK AND SUSIE GRAETZ
Bottom: From below Beartop Lookout, the North Fork of the Sun Valley.   RICK AND SUSIE GRAETZ

Top: Looking south from the Gates Park Ranger Station. RICK AND SUSIE GRAETZ
Bottom: The Danaher River and Meadows looking south. RICK AND SUSIE GRAETZ

Above the Danaher River and Meadows looking north toward the South Fork of the Flathead. RICK AND SUSIE GRAETZ

The headwaters of the North Fork of Birch Creek.   DOUGLASS DYE

Top: Carmine Peak and Sapphire Lake near the Holland Lake Trail into the Bob. DOUGLASS DYE
Bottom: Big Salmon Lake. RICK AND SUSIE GRAETZ

Trilobite Lakes looking southwest toward Pentagon Mountain.   BOB COONEY

Top: Looking down Seedling Creek.   BILL CUNNINGHAM
Bottom: Slategoat Mountain from Redhead Peak.   BILL CUNNINGHAM

Top: The Flathead Alps.   RICK AND SUSIE GRAETZ
Bottom: A glacier lives on the east slopes of Holland Peak.   RICK AND SUSIE GRAETZ

THE SCAPEGOAT STORY
by Rick and Susie Graetz

When any swath of land enters the National Wilderness Preservation system it is cause for celebration. On August 20, 1972, the U.S. Congress passed Public Law 92-395 and Montana's Scapegoat north of Lincoln gained this lofty designation. Now, on the occasion of its 30th birthday, is a time to take a look back with great pride, for the Scapegoat is a special case. This is a citizen's Wilderness, and it became reality in the face of stiff U.S. Forest Service opposition. The protection gained was the result of an immense amount of public outcry and involvement. Voices from both sides of the political aisle lined up to support it.

The struggle is a colorful and heart warming story. If it hadn't played out, the nation would have lost forever a cherished piece of her heritage.

When compared to other Montana wilderness topography, the Scapegoat doesn't quite stack up as high on the majestic scenery scale, as it features only one geologic masterpiece. Simply put, it is a pleasing wilderness, providing easy access and a wonderful wild country experience. Well before it garnered national attention, generations of folks from Lincoln, Helena, Great Falls, Missoula and other nearby Montana communities found enjoyment and solitude in what was known to all as the Lincoln Backcountry. Its unroaded and untrammeled character added to the rugged individualism of those who chose Lincoln, an isolated place up until the late 1950s, as home.

The original Lincoln Backcountry was a 75,000-acre stretch of undeveloped Helena National Forest administered lands. The boundary reached south to within 12 miles of Lincoln and on the north touched the fabled Bob Marshall Wilderness. The 240,000-acre designated Wilderness of today sprawls over an area straddling the Continental Divide and reaching out to the inner segments of the southern Rocky Mountain Front. A landscape designated on its own as a wilderness, it is part of the greater Bob Marshall country consisting of the Scapegoat, Bob Marshall and Great Bear wilderness areas. This, the crown jewel of America's wild assets, contains 1.5 million priceless acres of protected mountains, meadows and forests and almost one million acres of surrounding de facto wilderness.

Scapegoat's dominant feature and the destination of most foot and horse travelers is its namesake, Scapegoat Mountain, a 9,204-foot-tall limestone reef. The peak itself is merely a bump on the magnificent three-mile-long massif honeycombed with caves. The reef's walls are sheer on almost all sides with access to the plateau restricted through the Green Fork drainage on the east and a few places on the west side. This somewhat level strip then rises on the north end to 9,079-foot Flint Mountain, the northern tip of the Scapegoat formation.

In the Green Fork, a stream pours out of the wall like a faucet. The cave behind it is reported to be about two miles long.

Half Moon Park, a beautiful place to camp, is immediately below the north and east side of Scapegoat Mountain. Here, an old burn has opened up views to the east. A great experience is to be snug in your tent when a summer storm is passing through. The thunder is amplified as it ricochets off the more than 1,000-foot-high walls of the amphitheater, creating a booming, percussion symphony.

Access to the Scapegoat is usually from the east by way of Elk Pass, the Dearborn River, Smith Creek or the Benchmark area. From the south and west side, approaches to the mountain and plateau are from the Danaher, the North Fork of the Blackfoot River and Lincoln. The Dobroda Creek headwater area, reached by trail from the North Fork of the Blackfoot Valley, offers one of the better ways to climb Scapegoat from the west. The same route also passes Tobacco Valley and McDonald Meadow, two scenic places south of the southern end of Scapegoat Mountain. A 1988 forest fire opened up much of this country.

Day walkers, horseback riders and weekend backpackers favor 9,411-foot Red Mountain, the highest summit in the Scapegoat and in the Bob Marshall country, and Heart Lake on its north side. The trailhead is reached by a road up Landers Fork, a tributary of the Blackfoot River east of Lincoln. Caribou Peak and Big Horn Lake, on the Continental Divide, are two other prominent Scapegoat landmarks. Several trails approach the peak and lake. One up the West Fork of Falls Creek on the Rocky Mountain Front is the most commonly used path.

A scramble up 8,401-foot Crown Mountain on the Rocky Mountain Front off of the Benchmark Road out of Augusta is rewarded by a great view of almost the entire bulk of Scapegoat Mountain and a good portion of the wilderness.

Three important waterways are born in the Scapegoat. Just south of the *"summit bump"* of Scapegoat Mountain, a spring gurgles out of the plateau's porous limestone and commences the flow of the Dearborn River. The Sun

River gathers its initial waters from the northeast side of Flint Mountain. Below the southern perimeter of the Scapegoat wall, Dobroda and Cooney creeks join to send the North Fork of the Blackfoot on its way to connect with the main river in the Blackfoot Valley.

According to Cecil Garland, *"patron saint"* of the Scapegoat, the prairie and Rocky Mountain Front around Augusta were at one time almost overrun with sheep. The sheepherders who summered their herds in the mountains named almost everything in the area, including Scapegoat Mountain.

Over the years, the small town of Lincoln became known as a base of operations for commercial packers and guides and an entry into the Lincoln Backcountry and Bob Marshall Wilderness. By word and deed, the regional and national reputations of the outfitters grew, and so did that of the land they worked in.

As the Lincoln District Ranger and the Supervisor of the Helena National Forest, two enthusiastic users and stewards of the Backcountry, who had both been on the job for nearly 20 years, prepared to retire in the late 1950s, new plans were being laid in the Forest Service Regional Office in Missoula to develop a system of roads that would open this special landscape to timber harvesting and campground construction. One could say the *"custodial"* era was ending and the *"management"* period was about to start.

In response to this threat, the Lincoln Backcountry Protection Association was formed to try to stop the development. Cecil Garland, who became the association's president in 1962, operated a hardware and sporting goods store in Lincoln and had worked four summers as a campground foreman for the Forest Service, resigning when he realized he could not pursue his goals from within the agency. Cecil would be primarily responsible for the Scapegoat Wilderness Act of 1972.

Garland remembers his reaction to the possible implementation of the development plan. *"A young Forest Service engineer came into our store in Lincoln and told me the USFS had abandoned a full survey of the road to the Lincoln Back Country and was now running only a flag line in their haste to build the road and quell the opposition. This young engineer in despair also told me that a bulldozer was sitting at the end of the road.*

I knew that time was short and called Congressman Jim Battin … I poured out my heart to him in a most pleading and earnest manner. He must have understood for he said he would help me … Battin then phoned Regional Forester Boyd Rasmussen and asked if he could have ten days to see what was going on up at Lincoln. Mr. Rasmussen replied no, the bulldozer was ready to go. Whereupon Congressman Battin told the Regional Forester that, 'By God, we had better have ten days.' At this time I believe the tide turned in our favor."

On April 19, 1963, some 300 people jammed into the small Community Hall in Lincoln to hear the Helena Forest Supervisor discuss the plan. Ground rules were set; supporters and opponents were to alternate and there would be no voice vote at the end of the meeting. Opponents of the development plan felt they had been *"gagged,"* and a *"near riot"* took place. The level of bitterness began to increase dramatically. The association's membership grew and it soon received the backing of the Montana Wilderness Association, the Wilderness Society and the Montana Fish and Game Department. Senator Lee Metcalf wrote the Forest Service asking it to delay the project. During the next several months, the Forest Service received no letters supporting its plan. The timber industry had expressed initial approval of the timber harvesting, but was heard from less and less as the controversy grew.

Cliff Merritt, the western regional representative of the Wilderness Society, used the Backcountry as a boy and when he saw a Forest Service road stake in his family's camping area he came to the sudden *"violent"* conclusion that they *"would build a road there over my dead body."* Merritt was a principal in the effort to get statutory protection for the area.

Robert Morgan, the new Forest Supervisor of the Helena National Forest, after looking over the situation, decided to postpone the development until *"absolutely necessary."* In a tactfully written memo in January 1964, Morgan told his superiors that although there was some passive support for the Forest Service's plan, *"we will get no active support from the man on the street."* Stating the plan was *"basically very sound,"* but that it was open to question on several points, he pointed out that the agency did not have a complete timber inventory of the area, that some timber of marginal quality had been sold, leaving an occasional *"mess"* behind, that neighboring National Forests were not fully coordinating their plans with Helena's and that the presently developed campgrounds around Lincoln were not being fully used. Morgan counseled the Regional Office that the Forest Service could probably win the Backcountry battle if it were willing to go all out, but in the process it would pay a severe public relations price, which might jeopardize some of its other programs in Montana.

This *"compromise attitude"* was not well received in the Regional Office which wanted to begin road construction as soon as possible. Over the next few years Morgan heard some rough words from his superiors, who questioned his loyalty and felt he had caved in to local demands. When the Lincoln Backcountry Protection Association met

Scapegoat Mountain in the Scapegoat Wilderness.   RICK AND SUSIE GRAETZ

in February 1964, Cecil Garland convinced its members that because they could not get the Forest Service to commit to a 10-year moratorium on the road building, the goal of their organization needed to be changed. Garland advocated calling for a wilderness designation for the area and that the wilderness be expanded to 200,000 acres to take in the Scapegoat Mountain region, which adjoined the Bob Marshall Wilderness.

In April 1965, Democratic Senators Lee Metcalf and Mike Mansfield introduced a bill to protect 75,000 acres of the Backcountry under the Wilderness Act. Montana conservationists approached Republican Congressman Jim Battin and told him about the Metcalf-Mansfield bill and that there were more acres that could be included. Cliff Merritt remembers, *"Big Jim had his feet on a desk and when he heard this, they came down fast . . . Jim saw this as an opportunity to leapfrog members of the other party."* Battin introduced his own bill calling for a 240,500-acre Lincoln-Scapegoat Wilderness. Metcalf and Mansfield who, Merritt concedes, had not been fully informed about the situation, soon switched their support to the Battin bill.

The Lincoln-Scapegoat bill was the first strictly citizen wilderness proposal made after the passage of the Wilderness Act, which mandated the Forest Service do a study of all their primitive areas for possible inclusion in the Wilderness System. Since it did not involve the expansion of a primitive area, the Lincoln-Scapegoat proposal was not explicitly covered by the study and review procedures of the Wilderness Act. The unique, potentially precedent-setting nature of the bill was one of the main reasons why its passage was delayed until 1972. The Forest Service leadership in Washington was concerned it would unleash similar proposals at a time when its work force was committed to finishing on schedule the primitive area reviews.

Tom Edwards, a former schoolteacher and outfitter in Ovando for many years, was an early member of the Lincoln Backcountry Association, he traveled twice to Washington, DC, to testify before congressional committees and gave this heartfelt eloquent testimony on behalf of the Lincoln-Scapegoat. *"Into this land of spiritual strength I have been privileged to guide on horseback literally thousands of people ... I have harvested a self-sustaining natural resource of the forest of vast importance. No one word will suffice to explain this resource, but let us call it the 'hush' of the land. This hush is infinitely more valuable to me than money or my business."*

As Bob Morgan later recalled, the 1968 hearings were *"disastrous"* for the Forest Service. Pointing to severe erosion caused by road construction in an area near the Lincoln-Scapegoat, Senator Metcalf testily asked Morgan how the Forest Service *"could justify that!"* Morgan could only reply, *"I can't."* Soon after the hearings, the Forest Service published a new plan for a 500,000-acre area, which included the Lincoln-Scapegoat. The plan called for some land to be administratively protected as *"backcountry"* and for the construction of a 75-mile scenic Continental Divide Highway through the Lincoln-Scapegoat. Local environmentalists were not placated.

The Forest Service was becoming annoyed over an issue, which refused to go away. In early 1969, this frustration moved Regional Forester Neal Rahm to tell a meeting of the agency's leaders that a *"backcountry"* land category, intermediate between complete wilderness and developed campgrounds, was needed. *"We have lost control and leadership in the sphere of Wilderness philosophy. Why? The Forest Service originated the concept in 1920, and practically, has been standing still since about 1937 . . . Why should a sporting goods and hardware dealer* [Cecil Garland] *in Lincoln, Montana, designate the boundaries for the 240,000-acre Lincoln Backcountry addition to the Bob Marshall? . . . If lines are to be drawn, we should be drawing them."* His remarks were the first indication that the Regional Office was bowing to the inevitability of wilderness designation for the Lincoln-Scapegoat.

One month after Rahm's remarks, Chief of the Forest Service Ed Cliff told the Senate Interior Committee that the Forest Service would take another look at the Lincoln-Scapegoat. Plans for development were now permanently on hold.

Cecil Garland relates that Congressman Battin asked him to draw up the boundaries for his wilderness bill. Over a bottle of cheap whiskey, Garland and Forest Service men Lloyd Reesman and Bob Brown drew the lines for the future Scapegoat Wilderness.

Two years later, the supervisors of the Helena, Lolo, and Lewis and Clark National Forests drafted a wilderness proposal, based on the boundaries recommended by these three *"cartographers"*, which the Regional Office accepted. The Senate passed the Scapegoat Wilderness bill in 1969 and sent it to the House, where it was accidentally referred to the Agriculture Committee rather than the Interior Committee, thus arousing the ire of Chairman Wayne Aspinall who may have suspected an attempt to circumvent him. When he finally received the bill, Aspinall delayed reporting it out because the US Geological Survey had not conducted a mineral survey of the area as called for by the Wilderness Act.

Cecil Garland recalls how Aspinall was persuaded to support the bill. *"I had just left the House Office Building and Congressman Wayne Aspinall, the powerful chairman of the Interior and Insular Affairs Committee; he had told me he would 'kill' my bill. I relayed this message to Senator Mike Mansfield who listened quietly and then said, 'Ceace, you go back to Montana and tell the folks we'll get the bill passed, that there'll be a wilderness there some day. Some day there will be something that Mr. Aspinall will want, and we'll be there.' We shook hands and I walked with him to the Senate floor where a great fight was being waged over Vietnam.*

"Later when Congressman Aspinall became fully committed to the passing of the bill, I asked him why he had decided to help us. His reply was, 'Son, you've got one powerful Senator,' and I knew what he meant. I knew Mike had not forgotten."

In 1972 the Scapegoat Wilderness became the first de facto wilderness to enter the National Wilderness Preservation System. As mentioned earlier, the Forest Service opposed the Lincoln-Scapegoat proposal because it did not want to disrupt its timetable for primitive area reviews. The Regional Office was also concerned that if the Backcountry Association were successful there would be petitions for numerous other de facto wildernesses surrounding the Bob Marshall Wilderness.

Several years after the passage of the Scapegoat Wilderness bill, Morgan, with the congratulations of the Regional Office, received an award from an environmental group for his part in preserving the Lincoln-Scapegoat area.

For decades the Forest Service had tried to insulate itself from local demands on the national forests in order to carry out its mandate to protect them in the national interest. These pressures usually came from groups that wanted to use them in ways that could have been detrimental to their long-term well-being. Environmental organizations and many in the general public supported the Forest Service when it resisted these demands. In the case of the Lincoln-Scapegoat, local pressure was applied, not to hurt the forest but to protect it completely. The Forest Service fought this demand in the same way that it would have fought demands to overcut or overgraze the area. The difference was that here the Forest Service was operating without public support.

This conclusion, however, must be qualified. A strongly professional organization, such as the Forest Service, is open to internal debate. Without the dissenting voices of Bob Morgan and the Lincoln District Rangers who served under him, roads would have been built in the Lincoln-Scapegoat long before the Scapegoat Wilderness Act of 1972.

FOREST RANGER 1907 ON THE ROCKY MOUNTAIN FRONT
By Clyde Fickes

Editors note: This piece is excerpted from a report Clyde Fickes wrote in May 1944. It appeared in Volume 1- Early Days In The Forest Service. His words are unedited and appear as he penned them. Fickes retired from the Forest Service in 1947. He died on Dec. 29, 1987, at age 103, from an accident on the dance floor.

I applied for work on the old Lewis & Clark National Forest in the spring of 1907. Appointed a Forest Guard on July 1st at $60 per month and supplying two horses, and myself I was assigned to a survey party on the Swan River. On July 23rd and 24th I took the Forest Ranger examination at Kalispell and was directed to go to the Hannan Gulch Ranger Station on the North Fork of the Sun River. It has always been my impression that I was not considered a very promising candidate for ranger by Acting Supervisor A.C. McCain, so he figured, *"I'll give this kid an assignment that he won't want to accept, or else he will never get to Sun River and we will be well rid of him."*

They gave me a badge, a USE BOOK, and a GREEN BOOK and told me *"When you get to Hannan, you can take charge of the Sun River District."* That's how I became a forest ranger in 1907.

Well, I fooled McCain. I had discussed with Ranger Jack Clack the possible routes to follow. He had suggested the best route for that time of year was to go up *"Big River"*, the Middle Fork of the Flathead, follow the railroad until I reached the east side, and then south across country, until I reached Sun River.

Leaving Kalispell on July 26th, with saddle and packhorses, I swam the South Fork (of the Flathead), which was high, and camped the first night at the old Fitzpatrick homestead about where the present highway bridge is located.

Most of the trail followed the tote road used in building the railroad back in the '90s, and there were places where the trail lay between the iron rails, which made travel by horse a little hazardous at times, as one never knew when a train would want to use the tracks. That second night on the trail, I camped about 3 or 4 miles east of Belton (West Glacier) on the old tote road grade near some cabins where there was good grass for the horses. The next day, I made it to Essex and camped for the night with Ranger Dick Bradley and his family.

In the morning the horses and I forded the *"Big River"* and even though the current was rather fast, we made it to the other side all right without much difficulty and proceeded up Bear Creek. Camped at the Phil Gypher place at his invitation, as there was good horse feed, and we were tired.

From Bear Creek we rode to the Lubec Ranger Station. Flies were real bad, giving the horses no rest, and I stayed over the next day to catch our breath. This was July 31, 1907. The problem now was to get across the Blackfeet Indian Reservation without having to go to Browning for a pass, therefore saving myself 2 days time. I camped at Wolf Plume's place on the Little Badger that night. I had worked on the cow roundup on the Reservation the year before and knew these Indians. They were camped on Wolf Plume's personal allotment putting up the hay. There were 5 or 6 tepees of them.

A couple of years before that, the Government had built for Chief Wolf Plume a two-room log cabin and partially furnished it, and it had never been used — even one night. The old man took me over and showed me the cabin and told me to camp in it for the night. I thanked the Chief and he said to me *"You got pass?"* I shook my head. He grinned, shook his head, and left me to make camp. There was a new six-hole Majestic stove in the cabin, and it had never had a fire in it. I didn't disturb its virginity!

I finally pulled into the little town of Dupuyer late that next night. We were tired; it had been a long, hot day. A manger full of hay looked good to my horses. I went looking for a steak for myself.

Late the next afternoon we arrived at Ranger Linc Hoy's ranch on Blackleaf Creek, spent the night and in the morning headed to the Godwin Ranch at the forks of Deep Creek. The horses had a good roll and spent the night in knee-deep grass.

Left Godwin Ranch about 9:30 A.M. and arrived at last at the Hannan Gulch Ranger Station at about 2:30 P.M. It was quite a climb down into the Sun River Canyon on a narrow winding trail, across bare slide areas made by deer and elk on slopes as steep as 60 degrees and more.

According to my diary, I had traveled some 190 miles in 10 days to reach my post of duty.

At Hannan, I found Assistant Ranger Henry Waldref in charge. He was an old-timer who had been appointed to patrol the forests and watch for forest fires for 6 months each year. He had a mining claim near Lincoln, and his 6 months' wages from the Forest Service were his winter's grubstake. Henry was camped in a tent along the creek, and I joined him there. To him the job was just a summer's outing. He had been in the hills for years; and

Forest guard Clyde P. Fickes in August of 1907 at the Hannan Gulch Ranger Station.
U.S. FOREST SERVICE PHOTO

I sure picked up a lot of handy ideas from him about life in the mountains and living off the back of a packhorse that have been useful to me all my life.

At that time, the Sun River Ranger District, with headquarters at the Hannan Gulch Ranger Station, included all of what is now called the Sun River drainage, (then called the North Fork), the Deep Creek drainage to the north and the Willow and Ford Creek drainages to the south. At that time, the stream running through the town of Augusta was known as the South Fork of the Sun River. What is now known as the South Fork of the Sun River was then known as the South Fork of the North Fork, and we also had the West Fork of the South Fork of the North Fork of the Sun River.

The Sun River country comprises some very interesting, not to say spectacular, topography. The river comes out of the mountains in a due east and west course some 8 or 9 miles and breaks through a series of five sawtooth-like reefs, ranging in elevation from 6,000 to 8,000 feet, with the river at 4,500 feet. The reefs are perpendicular on the east face and at a 45 to 60 degree angle on the west. Looks just like a row of sawteeth. At the junction of the North and South Forks, the river runs due north and south for some 45 to 50 miles and forms a beautiful valley with many open parks and side streams which head up against the Continental Divide on the west, part of which is known as the Chinese Wall, as spectacular a piece of country as you will see anywhere.

Natives of the area are brown, black and grizzly bear; blacktailed deer; elk; moose; mountain sheep and goat; and the usual run of mountain small fry. Cattle grazing was permitted on all the Sun River Ranger District except the West Fork of the South Fork and Pretty Prairie, which was reserved for winter elk feed. In May 1908, I counted and estimated that 500 to 600 elk wintered on the West Fork licks and vicinity. That was about all the elk in that area at that time.

The business of the district, which included all the forest from Deep Creek on the north to Ford Creek on the south, included 10 or 12 grazing permits for cattle on the upper North Fork, Beaver Creek, Woods Creek, Ford and Willow Creeks and along the boundary south of the North Fork. Also there were a few free use permits for wood on Willow Creek. A typical entry in my diary for August 13th reads: *"Rode up Beaver Creek road to Willow Creek, crossed over to Ford Creek and then rode NE to Witmer's ranch. Range along Beaver Creek getting short. Posted 4 fire warnings on Beaver Creek. No fires. 8 to 5."*

On September 30th, notice was received from Supervisor Bunker of Kalispell that a ranger meeting would be held at the mouth of White River on the South Fork of the Flathead River from October 14–18. The supervisor had just returned from a six month detail to Washington and I guess he wanted to see if his rangers could get around in the mountains. Eustace A. Woods, who was the ranger on the old Dearborn District and on occasion known as *"Useless"* to his close friends, was in town the same time I was and we agreed that, with four others, we would assemble at the mouth of the West Fork of the South Fork and trail over the Continental Divide together. Only one of the group had been over the route with a hunting party and was to be the guide. I call it a *"route"* advisedly, because there was no such thing as a located trail except along the main river. The appointed day of our meeting for departure was October 8th, but due to circumstances I could not get there.

On the morning of October 9th, Linc Hay, the ranger from Teton District and I left Hannan and camped at the beaver dams on the West Fork. The others had not waited for us so it was a case of finding our own trail over the divide. My diary for October 10th reads, *"moved up West Fork Trail, camped on top of the divide under the cliffs. Jumped about five miles of logs. Bum trail."* The next day we pulled down to the mouth of White River to be the first arrivals at the meeting site. Woods and the others had stopped to try to get some elk meat, but failed to do so.

All in all, nearly 20 rangers and guides gathered here to meet with Supervisor Bunker and Inspector D.C. Harrison from Washington D.C. Like all its successors, the ranger meeting on White River was mostly talk. We also did a Ranger Station survey under the direction of Inspector Harrison and on the third day, all moved down the river to Black Bear where a new cabin was being built for the ranger headquarters.

Snow was beginning to cover the high country so those from the east side — some nine of us — pulled out for home. No one wanted to buck the logs on the West Fork, so we went up to the Danaher Ranch and crossed through Scapegoat Pass and some 16 or 18 inches of snow.

On November 6th, I received a notice from the Civil Service Commission that I had passed the ranger examination and was eligible for appointment. On July 1, I had been appointed a forest guard at $720 per annum, promoted to $900 on August 1, appointed an assistant forest ranger on November 11 at $900 and on January 1, 1908, promoted to deputy forest ranger at $1,000.

The Hannan Ranger Station consisted of an old log cabin, 16x20, and dirt roof, a 14x16 hewn-log cabin with box corners, a log barn, corral, hay meadow and pasture — all taken from a former homesteader or squatter named Jim Hannan, who allegedly operated a station on the old Oregon-Montana horse rustling trail. The story is that Jim also liked beef steaks and occasionally butchered a steer, regardless of whose brand it might bear. Seems like the neighboring ranchers, led by one of the largest cow owners in the Sun River country, surrounded Jim in his old cabin and convinced him with a few *"Winchester salutes"* that it would be advisable to do a little dickering if he wanted to continue life's journey. Bullet holes were still evident when I occupied the cabin. Old Jim agreed to leave the country and not come back. Shortly after that, maybe 2 or 3 years later, the Government pre-empted it for use of us Forest Rangers.

For a Ranger Station, no more isolated or lonesome spot could have been found. Visitors were practically unheard of for months at a time. The nearest neighbor was Johnny Mortimer who homesteaded in the gulch named for him. Johnny was a recluse and a bachelor. He never went to town. He had complete surveillance of all approaches. If he was not in the mood and a visitor approached, he would simply fade away into the rocky cliffs behind the cabin and would not come out until the visitor left. Whenever I was going to Augusta, I would let him know. He would give me a list of anything he needed, and I always picked up any mail for him. Several old-time friends paid him periodic visits. Sometimes one of them would stay all night at the cabin, but Johnny would not come in.

About the most convenient facility connected with the Sun River District was the built-in bathtub with hot and cold running medicated water. There was a warm, almost hot, mineral spring at the forks of the North and South Fork. Over the years users of the spring had dug out a sizable pool. There was a cave where the water came out. I took advantage of this convenience whenever possible. I was told by some of the old-timers that in the '90s, in the late summer and early fall, a hundred or more folks from as far down as Great Falls would be camped at the springs. It was a beautiful spot until the Reclamation outfit ruined it with Gibson dam. In the fall of 1907 I helped build a beautiful two-room log cabin on the flat just below the spring. When Gibson Dam was built, the cabin was moved up to Arsenic Creek and burned in the 1919 fire. Incidentally, there was a double log cabin on Arsenic Creek known as the Choteau or Medicine Cabin, built by some Choteau men and used as a hunting camp in the fall. It was a convenient stopping place for all of us travelers.

What about the forest fires? Well, there just weren't any. I do not recall that we had any lightning to speak of all that summer, and it was plenty hot at times. Also, there were not very many people roaming around in the hills.

Looking north up Hannan Gulch at the newly erected flag pole at the Hannan Gulch Ranger Sation in 1908. U.S. FOREST SERVICE PHOTO

When I left Kalispell, my equipment consisted of a regular stock saddle with a blanket and bridle and a sawbuck packsaddle with a blanket and saddle pad, a pair of canvas alforjas (pack bags), a halter, and a lead rope for the packhorse. Camp equipment, consisting of two long-handled fry pans, three tin plates, coffee pot, table knives, forks and spoons, a hunting knife in scabbard, a .32 Special 1894 Winchester rifle with leather scabbard, my camp bed, and extra clothes, a yellow Fish brand slicker (raincoat to you) and a canvas pack cover 7x7.

My food supply consisted of a slab of Winchester bacon, 10 pounds flour, can of baking powder, salt, sugar, canned tomatoes, corn, string beans and milk-three of each. This stuff made a packhorse's load about 180 pounds. It was packed in the alforjas, which made two side packs for the packhorses, and the bed folded into a top pack with the canvas pack over it-rain and dust proof. Then I threw a diamond hitch (the one-man diamond which Jack Clack showed me) over the canvas cover, and we were ready to travel. The saddle horse carried the rifle in a leather scabbard, which hung from the saddle horn, my slicker, and me, which spent in travel with this kind of an outfit. Each individual used his own variation according to personal ideas and desires.

Cooking was done over an open fire, and you soon became accustomed to a regular routine of setting up camp. First, the horses were turned out to graze. Maybe you hobbled them or picketed one and turned the others loose to graze. Then you rustled some dry wood, selected a place downwind for your campfire, and got the fire started. Then you set up camp. Most of us carried a 7x9 tent with 18-inch sidewalls; this was pitched in a convenient dry place. The bedroll was spread over fir boughs, if you were inclined to luxury. By that time, the fire had burned down to a good bed of coals (only tenderfeet attempt to cook over a blazing fire). You ate, washed dishes, smoked a pipe or two or a cigarette, took a good look at the horses and probably, just before bedding down, decided for various reasons — poor feed, stormy weather prospects — to catch the horses and tie them up for the night. For various reasons, known only to a horse, they will take off during the night; and you have a long walk to find them. Sometimes you don't find them for 3 or 4 days; that's hard on the legs, not to mention your temper. In the morning you start a fire, check the horses, fix breakfast, pack up, bring in the horses, saddle up, and you are on your way.

In those early days you probably spent an hour or two cutting logs out of the trail or just clearing the way to get through to where you wanted to go. That was the way you lived in the field, as it is sometimes referred to. Old Henry Waldref had a homemade sheet iron folding stove that he packed with him. On a cold wet night, it would make a 7x9 tent almost luxurious living. Oh yes, most of us packed a sourdough can with us at all times. Couldn't live without it!

So went the life of a forest ranger in 1907–08.

AN INCREDIBLE HIKE
by Bob Cooney

Editor's note: Hazel, often referred to as 'Pinnacle Paul,' was well known by all who visited the North Fork Sun River country. Cooney told us that Paul hiked into the Sun River Mountains from his home north of Choteau in 1920 and stayed for nearly 60 years. During the summers he worked for the Forest Service constructing and maintaining trails, building field cabins, fighting fires and manning lookouts. His summer headquarters was the wilderness station at Gates Park on the North Fork of the Sun. His winters were spent as a caretaker of a remote dude ranch at the head of Gibson Lake on the edge of the Bob Marshall Wilderness, many miles from the nearest road; he lived by himself. The following is an excerpt from Bob Cooney's article of an amazing trip Paul made through parts of the wilderness in the early 1930s.

I am sure every mountain range has its stories of extraordinary hikes and I often think of one up along the Continental Divide in early December quite a while ago.

L. J. Howard, a forest ranger, and I were on elk patrol in the Bob Marshall Wilderness. Paul Hazel, who had spent much of his life up there, was helping us. He was an exceptional hiker.

We had spent the night at a little cabin on Cabin Creek on the North Fork of the Sun River. Our plan was to cover the winter elk range on the North Fork up to Gates Park that day. Snow was still fairly light along the river, so we weren't using snowshoes. Each of us planned to cover a different area and meet that evening at Gates Park.

We had no idea what sort of ordeal lay ahead for Paul as we parted that morning. He was to cross the river and go up Moose Creek several miles, check on any game, take snow-depth readings and head north through the timber to the Gates Park cabin.

L. J. and I got in to camp around dusk. There was no Paul. We waited to eat supper and still no Paul. He was a superb woodsman and knew the area intimately. We couldn't imagine what might have happened. Much as we wanted to get out there, we believed it would be best to wait till daylight to start a search for him.

It was well after midnight when the Forest phone jingled. The only line working at that time was one to the Spotted Bear Ranger Station way over on the South Fork of the Flathead River. It was Paul. He said he was calling from the old iron field phone up on the Continental Divide on Spotted Bear Pass.

He had found an unexpectedly large band of elk up Moose Creek. Tracks indicated they might have recently migrated across the Divide from the White River area. Paul thought it was essential to our work to verify this. So he headed on up Moose Creek. It was many miles to the Chinese Wall and the snow got deeper the higher he went. He found the snow so deep along the base of the Wall that he believed it would be better to get up on top to head north to the pass he wanted to check. He managed to work his way up through the steep little pass at the head of Moose Creek. It was getting dark up there on top. He found the wind had blown the crest fairly free of snow. There was no trail and he had no light, but he made his way several miles along the top of the Continental Divide to an elk migration trail just south of Larch Hill. To think about how he got down off that end of the Wall through the snow cornices makes me shudder. In the dim light of the stars he could make out by tracks that a large group of elk recently had crossed the pass from the west side of the Continental Divide. This was the information he had worked so hard to verify.

He then made his way through deep snow around the shoulder of Larch Hill and on to the field phone at Spotted Bear Pass. There were still many miles to go to our camp down Rock Creek through heavy timber and snow. On the phone we had suggested he find a sheltered place, build a fire and wait till daylight. We said we would head up that way to give him a hand by breaking trail.

We were just about to leave when we saw Paul come out of the timber across the meadow. The Gates Park cabin, in the first gray light of the morning with smoke drifting out of the chimney must have looked good to Paul. I know he looked mighty good to us.

L. J. and I tried to figure how far he had hiked that day and night. He had traveled up Moose Creek much of the way in the snow without snowshoes. He had searched his way in the dark with no light along the crest of the Chinese Wall on the Continental Divide. There was no trail and a thousand-foot drop off to the east. Then there were all those miles down Rock Creek. He had hiked through deep timber where it was so dark that here and there he had to feel for blazes on the trees to make sure he was still on the snow covered trail.

He must have hiked nearly 40 miles. Paul has always been a man of few words. His only reference to the difficulty of the trip was his comment after breakfast: *I guess maybe I'll stay in today and wash some clothes.*

HISTORY NOTES: A COLLECTION
compiled by Rick and Susie Graetz

Charlie Russell, the well-known western artist, frequently used to hunt in the Sun River country and often camped in the Wrong Creek area.

The current-day Klick guest ranch, known as the K-Bar-L, located near the confluence of the North and South Forks of the Sun River, was at one time called the Allan Ranch. Originally, it was 40 acres of deeded land given to a civil war veteran. Ralph Allan initially was involved with Bruce Neal in establishing an early-day outfitting business. Later on, Allan developed the property that is now owned by the Klicks. At the same time, Bruce Neal homesteaded near this area at Scattering Springs.

Around 1930, a CCC group was working near Hahn Creek to build a landing strip. The project was never completed, nor was the airstrip ever used.

It is hard to imagine sheep grazing in the wilderness. The route between the North Fork cabin and the North Fork of the Blackfoot, the Kutenai Creek and the Scapegoat area was used for early-day sheep drives. Sheep also frequented the Tobacco Valley south of this region near Scapegoat Mountain and the Drivefork Area. Sheepherders originally built the Carmichael cabin, marked on many maps.

Charlie *"Kid"* Young for whom Youngs Creek was named was an early-day surveyor and trapper who stayed in the wilderness country during the winter and came out in the spring on the high water.

Near Big Prairie, there is a grave for a little girl with the last name of Roush. In about 1925, she became quite ill and her father snowshoed out to Missoula for medicine. Upon his return, he found that his daughter had died.

In 1912, a phone line was put up along the North Fork of the Sun to the Gates Park Station. Just south of there, at Two Shacks Flat, were two old cabins used by woodcutters, so that's how the place got its name.

In about 1910, a railway survey was conducted up along the Sun River. The route was projected to go up the North Fork of the Sun, over Sun River Pass, down Bowl Creek to the Middle Fork of the Flathead and out to Coram. Of course this bizarre idea never came about.

Chick Grimsley worked in the Middle Fork country in the 1880s and often used wickiups for his camping. These are nothing more than crude lean-tos formed by poles leaned against trees for shelter. Some are still to be found.

The Upper South Fork of the Flathead River experienced heavy trapping up until the 1930s, but it then tapered off. Many old, crude trapper's cabins or their remains still exist.

The headwaters country of Badger Creek was one of the favorite hunting areas of Gifford Pinchot, a giant in Forest Service history. He was known to frequent the area in the early 1900s.

During the 1929 season, a fire lookout ranger on Desert Mountain in the northern part of the Bob Marshall country just south of Glacier Park, counted among his experiences seeing two square miles on one side of his mountain swept clean by flames in the short period needed for him to sprint 200 yards.

Reliable observers have reported somewhat peculiar conditions on high mountaintops just preceding violent electric storms. A certain scientist recounts vividly an experience on Great Northern Mountain, in the Great Bear, when his party found rifles, geologic picks and other metallic instruments emitting sparks visible in full daylight. One of the picks is reportedly still there, left by the owner who quickly dropped it as the party ran for a nearby glacier to lie close to the ice until the approaching thunderstorm had passed.

Early Attempts at Settlement

In 1899, H.B. Ayres, of the Division of Geography and Forestry of the Department of the Interior, made a survey of what was then the Lewis and Clark Reserve. While traveling in the North Fork of the Sun River, he mentioned that there was some grazing going on and a few cabins were visible. He also had the opportunity to travel in the Danaher Meadows area in the upper reaches of the South Fork of the Flathead.

Tom Danaher and A.P. McCrea, most likely the first white men to settle on the South Fork, homesteaded 160 acres each in 1898. They built several structures, including houses and barns and put in hay and grazed cattle and horses. Climate, poor yields of hay for their stock, as well as accessibility to the outside world caused McCrea to abandon his homestead and in 1907, Danaher sold his land to the Hunt Club of Missoula. The Hunt Club had planned to raise horses on the ranch, but were affected by the same conditions as the two homesteaders. Sam O. Acuff eventually took over ownership. Later, the Forest Service bought him out.

The Ralston brothers at one time, tried to develop a coal mine somewhere along the Middle Fork of the Flathead River. The attempt was unsuccessful.

There were other homesteads filed in what is now wilderness. In 1911, the Gates Park area was homesteaded and in 1913, several other tracts in the Danaher were filed upon, but were not occupied. Climatic conditions and perhaps the fires of 1910, which burned much of the present wilderness area, probably influenced the low interest.

In 1915, David H. Lewis, the District Ranger of the Big Prairie Ranger District compiled an agriculture report on the Upper South Fork of the Flathead. In essence his report said that the combination of severe winters, a short growing season, a limited number of farming acres, the high cost of developing access and the minimal chances of agriculture successes should dictate that this land is not suitable for agricultural activities. He recommended that all lands south of Black Bear Creek be closed to entry under the Forest Homestead Act. He also pointed out that the area's fish and wildlife values would be jeopardized by settlement. He felt that the area was of greater importance for attracting hunters and fisherman.

Lewis also pointed out *"the present routes of travel are trails, where it is only possible to use saddle and pack horses. The distance from Corum, a Flag Station on the Great Northern Railway, to Black Bear is 70 miles, to White River 83 miles and to Big Prairie 91 miles. The distance from Ovando, to the following localities is as follows: Danaher Creek 40 miles, Basin Creek 50 miles, Big Prairie 60 miles, White River 68 miles and Black Bear 81 miles. There are 15 miles of wagon road leading out from Ovando connecting with the trail to Danaher. The trails leading into this country from Corum and Ovando were constructed by the Forest Service and are very fair trails. They are the only routes of travel to the Upper South Fork."*

The Early Days
by Charlie Shaw

Editor's note: Charlie S. Shaw put together a publication in the early 1960s for the Forest Service titled The Flathead Story. Shaw worked for more than 31 years with the Forest Service beginning in the 1920s. Thirty of the years were spent in the areas of the South and Middle Forks of the Flathead River, now in the Bob Marshall Wilderness. This publication covered much of the Flathead National Forest. The excerpts that follow are about the Bob Marshall country only. We have taken them exactly as Shaw presented them in his fine publication.

In 1898, Forest Service Rangers roamed the mountainous terrain of the Flathead at a salary of $60 per month. They had to supply their own horses, bedrolls, and subsistence out of this pay. Examinations for Forest Rangers and examinations for Forest Supervisors were separate. It was possible, by passing the examination, to be appointed Supervisor without having worked for the Forest Service or having had technical training in forestry. The pay was $75 per month. The following is an excerpt of a typical appointment letter. *"Frank Opalka, May 23, 1906. You have been appointed a Forest Guard at $60 per month to take effect June 1. On June 1 you will report to Ranger Sullivan at the U.S. cabin near Coram with your outfit and supplies for 2 months. Tools and tents will be furnished by the Service. You will work under the direction of Ranger Sullivan on the South Fork of the Flathead. Unless otherwise ordered by this office, you will not leave the Reserve before July 31."*

Col. Sievers, U.S. Army, made a trip through the South Fork of the Flathead River in the early 1870s, perhaps as early as 1874. The party was seeking a route for a railroad into this area. They killed an elk at Mud Lake for camp meat. This was the first report of elk in the Flathead country.

In 1903, the first constructed Forest Service trail extended from Ovando to the Danaher Basin, a distance of 21 miles.

In 1905, Flathead National Forest headquarters were moved from Ovando to a one room in the Conrad Bank Building in Kalispell. Rent was $10 per month including heat. Supervisor Page S. Bunker asked for a clerk to remain in the office during his absence. He preferred a man who could use a typewriter.

In 1906, the first Spotted Bear Ranger Station was built by John Sullivan.

In 1908, the Lewis and Clark National Forest was divided into two National Forests: Blackfeet and the Flathead. Forest Service crews constructed the first telephone line; the line went from Kalispell and Coram. In 1910, a telephone line was completed to Spotted Bear. In 1912, a telephone line was extended to Big Prairie. In 1914, the lookout was constructed on

Spotted Bear Mountain. It was used as an observation tower until it was replaced in 1933.

In 1925, Forest Rangers A. E. Hutchinson, Roy Hutchinson, and Al Austin found the frozen body of a hermit trapper named Marshall in his cabin on Cabin Creek in the South Fork drainage. Marshall had ended his life with a pistol. He had been dead for more than a month when the Rangers discovered his body in February. They made a sled and hauled the frozen corpse 35 miles over the snow-covered mountains to Ovando.

In 1939, the first air drop of a Flathead National Forest fire camp was made in the Bunker Creek drainage.

In 1953, the 46-mile road along the west side of the Hungry Horse Reservoir was completed by the Bureau of Reclamation at a cost of $2 million dollars.

On June 1, 1898, Gust Moser at Ovando received his appointment as Forest Supervisor of the northern division of the then Lewis and Clark Forest Reserve through J.B. Collins, Forest Superintendent, Missoula, Department of the Interior, General Land Office.

Early Rangers furnished the pack stock required to move their provisions and supplies. But as the Forest Service grew, so did the job of packing. Soon the Forest Service had its own pack stock, principally horses, and hired the men to pack them.

All saddles were *"sawbucks"*; the *"diamond hitch"* was used extensively. Usually two men with from 15 to 20 head of horses worked together on long trips, such as from Coram to Big Prairie, which required about 2 weeks for a round trip. They didn't usually tail them together; they just herded them down the trail, one man on horseback up front and the other bringing up the rear. They camped in any spot with water and grass for the horses. Horses were turned loose in the hopes the men could find them the next morning. These were long, hard days. The standard of living at some of these camps was not very high. It was not very pleasant when it rained or snowed. Packing continued this way until the 1920s, when the mules started to replace the horses and the Decker packsaddles replaced the sawbucks for general use In the Forest Service, the diamond hitch went out with the sawbucks. They were replaced by using *"manta"* on side packs, which was more convenient than top packs and the diamond hitch, and they are easier on the animal. The last diamond hitch that I can remember seeing *"thrown"* in the Forest Service was in 1928.

Mule trains also brought more standardized packing. Mules were tied together in a string: eight mules, a *"bell mare."* and the packer's saddle horse.

Early settlers took title to practically all the suitable land up on the North Fork of the Flathead and much of the land in the Swan Valley. Most of these areas remain in private ownership today. Except for the upper South Fork on Danaher Creek, the South Fork and the Middle Fork above the railroad were never filed on by these adventurous pioneers. Two homesteads of 160 acres each were filed in 1898 by Thomas Danaher and A.B. McCrea. These homesteads were purchased by the Federal Government after the area was included in the South Fork Primitive Area. Northern Pacific Railway land grants in the Upper South Fork were all acquired by land exchange and are now part of the Flathead National Forest.

Mickey Wagoner's homestead, above Martin City, was the farthest up the South Fork. There were no homesteads on the Middle Fork River above Bear Creek.

A special-use permit was granted on Morrison Creek, about a mile above the Three Forks cabin, in the early 1920s to a Denver attorney named Hunter. The Hunter family used it as a summer home until 1928. Today only the ruins of the cabin's rock chimney remain.

About 1919, a special-use permit was issued on Hahn Creek, a branch of Young's Creek, on the upper South Fork above Big Prairie, to Ruby Kirchbalm. After divorcing her rich physician-husband, Ruby fell in love with the *"great out-of-doors."* She bought a string of horses, hired *"Smokey"* Denow as a packer, and started a packing business. Ruby proved an able packer. Teamed with *"Smokey"*, a rugged, Paul Bunyan type, Ruby Kirchbalm moved a lot of freight in the Flathead country. Often they packed for the Forest Service in the summer. They wintered their stock in the upper South Fork for several years. After five years, Ruby's interest in the backcountry paled. She returned to the east in 1924.

Just east of the Forest Service's Hahn Creek administrative site cabin, you can still see the cement *"pad"* where Ruby's cabin was built more than 45 years ago.

About 1919, Joe Murphy of Ovando started packing hunters into the South Fork. He always camped on the open flats below Holbrook Creek across the South Fork from White River. Today, this area is known as Murphy Flats. The Forest Service issued Murphy a special-use permit for the area in 1922. He built some nice log cabins and a lodge. They served as his hunting headquarters until about 1937 when the permit was terminated by mutual agreement. The camp was then in the South Fork Primitive Area. The Murphy's sons still use the land as their headquarters when in the area with fishing and hunting parties, but the buildings are gone.

In the fall of 1949, when the Murphys were breaking camp near the end of the hunting season, their party consisted of 22 hunters, not counting Murphy's help. Each hunter had an elk. Murphy, his sons, and packers moved this party and meat all in one trip. Each hunter had a saddle horse. Murphy's outfit is perhaps the largest and best that has used the Bob Marshall Wilderness for any length of time. Joe Murphy personally used this same area for 45 continuous years.

The Murphy and Kirckba1m special-use permits — first issued over 40 years ago — are the only ones ever issued on the South Fork above Spotted Bear. Creation of the South Fork Primitive Area in 1931, and subsequently the Bob Marshall Wilderness in 1941, precludes any permanent camps in this area.

Homesteading on the Great Plains and railroad construction brought a local demand for lumber and railroad ties. In about 1886, Charles Biggs and others built a wagon road from what is now Hannah Gulch up Sun River to Gates Park. This is now about 14 miles inside the Bob Marshall Wilderness. They proceeded to cut railroad ties on Headquarters Creek and Biggs Creek and float them down the North Fork of the Sun River. Their main camp was on Headquarters Creek, not far from Gates Park. They cut 200,000 ties and hauled out 25,000 cords of fuel wood between 1886 and 1899. The operation was not economical due to insufficient water at times in Sun River and the long distance to market.

Construction of Gibson Dam on the Sun River above Hannan Gulch in 1929 inundated several miles of the lower end of this road. The 14 miles of road in the wilderness have now grown over; the logging scars have healed and most of the stumps are no longer in evidence. It is again a true wilderness. However, following the logging operations near Gates Park, a homestead claim was filed in 1911. It was never occupied. In 1913, four tracts of land in the Danaher Basin were homesteaded beside the Danaher and McCrea homesteads of 1898. They were filed but never occupied. Climatic conditions, together with the long winters and distance to market over a rough trail, made farming and stockraising in these areas uneconomical.

In the late 1940s and early 1950s, extensive exploration by gas and oil interests brought pressure on the Forest Service for leases in the wilderness. The Forest Service objected to this exploitation as incompatible with wilderness preservation. The Bureau of Land Management Department of interior (the granting agency), agreed with the Forest Service. As a result, no leases were ever granted in the wilderness.

In November 1949, a severe windstorm blew down a large volume of timber in the Flathead National Forest. Englemann spruce, being quite shallowly rooted, was especially vulnerable to a storm of this intensity. Fallen timber provides an opportunity for insects to breed and incubate, especially the spruce beetle. An epidemic of these insects struck most of the major drainages containing spruce, including Bunker Creek, just north and outside of the proclaimed boundary of the Bob Marshall Wilderness.

While wildlife in the National Forest was always a concern of the early-day rangers, wildlife studies were not started until the early 1920s. Rangers traveled in pairs on snowshoe, usually with provisions and supplies on their backs. Cabins were few and far between; they made camp where night overtook them. These trips took from two to three weeks. Rangers counted the game in the areas they passed through and noted the condition of the wildlife and the condition of the winter range. They also checked for poaching or illegal trapping. Dog teams were tried as means of transporting supplies on these game-study trips. These dogs and sleds, however, did not prove to be very satisfactory because much of the travel was on steep side slopes and through the brush off the trail. This system was soon abandoned.

The building of more cabins added to the convenience of these trips. Until 1928, the Three Forks cabin was the only building on the Middle Fork. Alen Calbick built this one and one-half-story log cabin in 1910. Lumber for the cabin was *"whip-sawed"* near the site. It was used until it was damaged by heavy snow in 1956.

These annual game trip reports showed that the game had increased beyond the carrying capacity of the winter range. Some of the Rangers who carried on these studies were A.E. Hutchinson, Al Austin, M.B. Mendenhall, Fred J. Neitzing, Tom Wiles, J. Roy Hutchinson, Henry Thol, and F.S. June (Forest Service employee). There may have been others I do not recall.

In the early 1930s, it was realized that the elk population was getting too large for the winter range. As a result, a more intensive study was initiated in the fall in 1933. Three crews were organized to spend the winter in the area to study the problem. One crew was headquartered at Big Prairie, one at Spotted Bear, and the third on the Middle Fork at Schaefer.

The crews, with 6 months' supplies, went into these areas in early November and did not come out until late the following April. There were no plans for receiving fresh supplies or mail. Each crew carried a short-wave battery-powered radio for contacting the Supervisor's Office in Kalispell. Sometimes these radios worked. Crews heard from their families through the Forest Supervisor. I learned one day that I was the father of a baby daughter and that my wife and daughter were doing fine.

These men went through the usual dangers and hardships that go along with winter traveling on snowshoes in the mountains: snowslides, breaking through the ice in crossing rivers, short on rations, getting caught in storms, the cold weather (one time at Spotted Bear it was 57 degrees below zero), and camping out in the snow. These were all taken in stride. Perhaps the fact that there was a national financial depression had something to do with the men taking all of this in stride.

These wildlife studies were continued, in much the same manner, for the next four winters. The situation was analyzed and steps were taken to do something about the overstocked winter elk range. Spotted Bear Game Preserve was eliminated in 1936. The Montana Fish & Game Department extended the 30-day season to 75 days. Odds did not favor such large numbers of game; the winter range was greatly reduced; and, of course, the elk herd was reduced principally by malnutrition.

Following the four winters of intensive studies, yearly winter game patrol trips were made by the Forest Service through the area until 1941–42. Then, the Montana Fish & Game Department put crews in the area for winter study.

In January and February of 1941, Ranger Leif Anderson and I went through the South Fork from Coram and, after taking side trips up the major drainages, came out 32 days later at Ovando. We traveled on skis.

Some bears are quite smart. According to a story told by a crew at Schafer in 1938 (Schafer was then just a tent camp), they were having some difficulty in keeping their bacon away from the bears. In itself, this is not unusual. They put a long pole over a pivot in a fashion similar to a child's "teeter-totter." On one end of the pole, they attached a box for the bacon. On the other end, they attached a box of rocks, heavy enough to keep the bacon in the air. The box with the bacon in it had a rope attached; this enabled the crew to pull the bacon down when they wished. It worked good. They thought they had solved the problem, until a new bear came to camp. He would climb up the inclining pole and, as he passed over the balance point, the bacon box end came to the ground. The bear would then jump to the ground and immediately the heavier rock box dropped to the ground, raising the bacon up again. After several attempts of this kind, the bear left. Now, the men were more sure than ever that their contraption was a success. But the bear had not given up. He returned with another bear. The second bear stole the bacon out of the box as the other bear brought it to the ground. Of course, the bears got into a fight, but they had the bacon.

The Monture Ranger Station
reprinted from Forest Service files

The first Monture Ranger Station was near Shoup Lake on property belonging to the Anaconda Copper Mining Company and the Northern Pacific Railroad. Before the Forest Service came into being in 1905, the area was called The Lewis and Clark Forest Reserve and administered by the General Land Office.

The headquarters for the southern half of the Reserve was Ovando. The purpose of the Monture station was to aid in fire control and it was not manned in the winter. There are few remaining records about the original Monture station, but it is known that a Supervisor Bliss built a two-story house and a pasture fence on Section 31, about two miles south of the present Monture Ranger Station. The fact that it was not government-owned land apparently did not disturb Bliss. And it didn't disturb the Northern Pacific or the A.C.M. either. They had logged the area in the late 1890s and probably considered the land useless to them until time for the next timber harvest in about sixty years.

By 1911, the Forest Service was leasing the land for $10 per year from the owners. This arrangement was making Forest Supervisor David H. Kinney uneasy. Kinney counted $1,325 in improvements on the property and the land could be sold out from under them at any time.

Furthermore, since the Lewis and Clark Forest Reserve had split up into National Forests in 1905 and the Monture Station was now part of the Missoula National Forest, land had been set aside elsewhere for a ranger station. Certain parcels of land were set aside in each ranger district in 1908 for *"administrative purposes"* such as grazing land or fire lookouts or ranger stations. The land set aside for the Monture Ranger Station was in Section 20, about two miles to the north.

In 1914 John R. Toole of the A.C.M. informed Forest Supervisor Rutledge Parker that a private party was interested in leasing the land at more than what the Forest Service was paying. Parker, commenting on the situation, said, *"It seems to me the government should own land in every case where the headquarters stations are situated.*

I am in favor of abandoning the present site and occupying the site which was originally set aside for a ranger station." And by 1920, a simple square cabin and some outbuildings had been built on the Section 20 land after the Forest Service cleared a space in the heavy timber.

The cabin served as ranger headquarters until 1927 when Seeley Lake Ranger Walt Robb and crew built the present station house and barn. Sometime between 1908 and 1927 the Ovando Ranger District was absorbed by the Seeley Lake District and the Monture outpost became part of the Seeley Lake Ranger District and is now a work center.

"Slippery Bill"
by Fred J. Neitzling former Supervisor, Flathead N.F.

At the turn of the century, one of the most colorful Rangers appointed for seasonal work was William H. Morrison, better known as *"Slippery Bill."* He provided his own headquarters at Summit and was responsible for the Middle Fork of Flathead River drainage.

In Grace Hansen's History of Flathead County — Great Northern Landmarks, she relates *"Long before the railroad came to Montana, a man named William H. Morrison held a squatter's right to a small piece of land at the Summit. When he heard that the Great Northern was extending its tracks through the Marias Pass, he installed a rosewood bar in his shack and was soon doing a flourishing business. The construction crews moved, but 'Slippery Bill,' as he was known, remained."*

"Bill was about 84 when he died, but before his death, he gave his small piece of land as a site for the obelisk in memory of Theodore Roosevelt. This monument, we hope, will be a landmark for many years to come, but we also hope that someone will keep alive the memory of the man who felt it an honor to give the government the land on which his shack was built, as a site for the memorial honoring the father of modem reforestation."

It was in the early '30s when Bill donated his 160 acres of *"squatter's right"* land and today, near the Roosevelt Memorial, a large native boulder carries a bronze plaque commemorating Mr. Morrison. Bill acquired his nickname as a result of his astuteness in a poker game. Around 1890, playing cards in a railroad construction camp at McCartyville — now a flag station called Fielding on the Great Northern Railway in the Middle Fork of Flathead River country, Bill won a great deal of money from the workers. In the later hours of the game, knowing he might be followed by his gambling associates and robbed of his winnings, Bill thought it unwise to leave with so much cash. Pocketing most of his money and leaving a small sum at his place at the card table, Bill excused himself, saying he would return in a few minutes. Once outside the room, he hurried away and didn't return, thus earning the title *"Slippery Bill."*

Quite late in his life, when he was still living at Summit, during the train's 10-minute stop to take on water and undergo routine inspection, the trainmen would give Bill a daily newspaper and chat with him. He was a tall, stately old man with a long white beard and he became well-known as a rustic philosopher. On the depot platform, it was routine for passengers to get out and promenade. An eastern woman approached old Bill and inquired, *"How do people make a living in this unpleasant, wind-swept, God-forsaken place?"* He replied, *"Lady, most of us make a comfortable living by minding our own business."*

Morrison Creek and Slippery Bill Mountain, a few miles south of Summit on the Flathead National Forest, are two features named after this early Forest Service pioneer.

The Pre-Region One Days
By Elers Koch

Editor's note: Koch, one of the U.S. Forest Service's innovative pioneers, was a native Montanan who took forestry degrees from Montana State College and Yale University. He entered government service in 1903, the beginning of a 40-year career that included 23 years as assistant district forester and chief of Division of Timber Management. Forest fire control techniques and formal training for firefighters were among Koch's many great contributions. He died in 1954.

In 1905, when Gifford Pinchot took over the Forest Reserves from the Land Offices, he took with them all the personnel — good, bad, and indifferent. The new Reserves, their proclamations fresh from the President's pen, had to be organized, and at the same time those already under organization inspected and checked up.

To that end, a lot of us young fellows in our twenties, with the vast experience of two years on the boundary job, were pitch forked by Pinchot into jobs as general inspectors and sent west to see what we could find out. Being a native son of Montana, my field of action was in Montana and Wyoming.

My first inspection of the old Lewis & Clark South in 1905, was an interesting job. This included the wilderness of the Blackfoot, Swan River, South Fork of the Flathead and the Sun River — and it was truly a wilderness at that time. Headquarters were at Ovando. The previous Supervisor had been Gus Moser, and many tales are told of his performances. It is alleged that he and his wife used to meet the rangers coming in for their monthly paychecks and mail, and that her wiles and other attractions, together with Gus' superior skill at poker, usually resulted in separating the rangers from most of their pay. Moser was succeeded by Bliss, who was Supervisor at the time of my inspection.

Bliss was a nice old man, but quite incompetent, and his only excursions to the forest were drives in a buckboard over the only road on the Reserve to Holland Lake in the head of the Swan. Fortunately for him, he had a ranger in Page Bunker. Bunker and I outfitted in Ovando with one pack horse and a saddle horse apiece. We rode up through the North Fork of the Blackfoot, across the range to the Dearborn, and north along the east side. Jack Clack (later in the Forest Service) was then buying government timber and operating a small mill west of Augusta. We went up the Teton and down the North Fork of Sun River. We tried to cross into White River, but a snowstorm drove us out and we went back over the Dearborn. It was interesting that we saw no big game on that month's trip, though we ate grouse nearly every day, knocking their heads off with our 30-30 rifles.

As a result of my inspection, Bliss was removed and Bunker made Supervisor and headquarters moved to Kalispell.

In 1906, I made another inspection of the Lewis & Clark south. I started from Kalispell with one of the rangers up the South Fork. By that time, the rangers had pushed a trail of sorts upriver as far as Spotted Bear, and from the head of the river down to Black Bear. Beyond that there was no trail, but we made it through on elk trails as best we could. Again, in a month's travel in the late fall we saw no big game. Bunker was doing good work opening up the country with trails so far as his limited funds permitted.

On the 1906 trip, I again crossed the main range and rode up the east side returning to Kalispell by a rugged trail along the Great Northern. I camped one night near Nyack, and during the night both my horses were run over and killed by a Great Northern train. I put in a claim, but through neglect in following it up the case expired by statue of limitation and I never collected a cent from the railway company.

The Lewis & Clark North in 1905 included all of what is now Glacier Park and the country northwest of Kalispell. F. N. Haines was Supervisor. Mr. Haines told me how he came to be appointed. He had been active in Republican politics in his home town in Indiana, and one day one of the Senators from that state called him in and said, *"Mr. Haines, I have two positions at my disposal. One is a postmastership, the other a Forest Supervisor in Montana. You can have either one."* Haines said he did not know a spruce tree from a pine, but he wanted to go west so he chose the supervisorship.

First Plane in the Bob

The first airplane landed in the Bob Marshall in 1928, a few months before aviation itself was 25 years old. Pioneer Missoula flyer Bob Johnson was at the controls of the OX-5 Swallow biplane that landed on a narrow, short Forest Service runway at Big Prairie. His passenger, Harry Gerard, worked as private secretary to W. A. Clark, Jr., and was joining his boss at the latter's fishing camp on Bartlett Creek.

In his biography of Bob Johnson, Fly the biggest Piece Back, Steve Smith offers the exciting account of this first flight, as it appeared in a Butte paper on August 9,1928.

PLANE THREADS WAY INTO WILD SECTION
Ship piloted by Bob Johnson of Missoula Lands
Harry Gerard at the Clark Camping Site

The heavily timbered country of the South Fork of the Flathead River north of Missoula, one of the wildest spots in the Northwest, with its sea of treetops and frowning crags and cliffs, has been invaded by airplane for the first time in history, with a landing being made on Big Prairie field, according to a forest ranger report completed in July.

Top: The Wall Creek cliff from Larch Hill.   RICK AND SUSIE GRAETZ
Bottom: The Danaher River and Meadows.   RICK AND SUSIE GRAETZ

Top: From the summit of Beartop, looking into the Headquarters Creek Canyon and Old Baldy. RICK AND SUSIE GRAETZ
Bottom: Looking southwest from Redhead Peak. BILL CUNNINGHAM

Top: Above Big River Meadows.   BILL CUNNINGHAM
Bottom: The South Fork of Birch Creek from the Continental Divide.   RICK AND SUSIE GRAETZ

Top: Half Moon Park below Scapegoat Mountain.   RICK AND SUSIE GRAETZ
Bottom: The Gooseberry Park Area and the beginnings of the Middle Fork of the Flathead River.   RICK AND SUSIE GRAETZ

Top: In Headquarters Pass looking west.   RICK AND SUSIE GRAETZ
Bottom: On top of Scapegoat Mountain.   RICK AND SUSIE GRAETZ

Top: In the South Fork of the Birch Creek area looking toward Mount Patrick Gass. RICK AND SUSIE GRAETZ
Bottom: Looking west through Gateway Gorge from above Big River Meadows. RICK AND SUSIE GRAETZ

Top: Sock Lake. RICK AND SUSIE GRAETZ
Bottom: The east face of Swan Peak. RICK AND SUSIE GRAETZ

Top: From the top of 8,873-foot Pentagon Mountain looking north along the Trilobite Range. RICK AND SUSIE GRAETZ
Bottom: Beaver Lake. BILL CUNNINGHAM

Top: The West Fork of the Sun River and Red Butte.   RICK AND SUSIE GRAETZ
Bottom: Old Baldy and Rocky Mountain Peak from Wapiti Ridge.   RICK AND SUSIE GRAETZ

129

Top: Todd and Rick Graetz hiking along the Chinese Wall. RICK AND SUSIE GRAETZ
*Bottom: The historic Beartop lookout. Pat McGuffin and Julie Butkis enjoy an
impromptu mountain top concert by fire-spotter Israel Tockman.* RICK AND SUSIE GRAETZ

Top: The Gates Park Ranger Station.   RICK AND SUSIE GRAETZ
Bottom: Dusty Crary leads his string down the east side of the Route Creek Pass Trail.   RICK AND SUSIE GRAETZ

Top: *Scapegoat Mountain.* RICK AND SUSIE GRAETZ
Bottom: *Looking down Moose Creek from the Chinese Wall.* RICK AND SUSIE GRAETZ

Top: From the top of the north end of the Chinese Wall looking north toward the Wall Creek Cliffs. RICK AND SUSIE GRAETZ
Bottom: Looking up Blind Creek from the North Fork of Birch Creek. RICK AND SUSIE GRAETZ

Top: From above the South Fork of the Flathead River looking at Big Salmon Lake and the Swan Range. RICK AND SUSIE GRAETZ
Bottom: Great Northern Mountain in the Great Bear Wilderness – Hungry Horse Lake in the distance. RICK AND SUSIE GRAETZ

Looking toward Swan Peak and the Swan Range.   RICK AND SUSIE GRAETZ

Climbers below Holland Peak on the Swan crest.   RICK AND SUSIE GRAETZ

The Danaher Ranger Station built in 1910. Photo taken in 1925. U.S. FOREST SERVICE PHOTO

Bob Johnson of Missoula, one of the intrepid flyers of the New York-to-Spokane air derby and aviation instructor at the Missoula airport, flew from the Garden City yesterday morning and in the course of an hour and ten minutes had located the camp of W.A. Clark, Jr., hidden far in the recesses of the forest, located the Big Prairie field, some 60 miles off the main road, and by dint of clever maneuvering among the pines and over them, landed his passenger, Harry Gerard of New York, guest of Mr. Clark, at his Salmon Lake summer home.

Forest Service Cabins
by Rick and Susie Graetz

In strategic and scattered locations throughout the wilderness, the U. S. Forest Service has constructed small cabins to support personnel patrolling the back country, for snow and animal survey work and for other administrative purposes. At Gates Park, Big Prairie, Spotted Bear and Benchmark, buildings are in place for use as work centers and, in the case of Spotted Bear, to serve as a ranger district. Until recently the Big Prairie site also was a ranger district.

There has been some question about the appropriateness of cabins in a wilderness setting. In some cases the pressure for removing these cabins has come from the Forest Service itself and from outfitters. The other side argues that valuable time and resources have gone into building these structures and a long-range study should be made before destroying them. They believe that time and money would be wasted by wilderness crews setting up camps if the cabins were destroyed. What happens to them remains to be seen. The following is a list of a few of these cabins, including their cost and the date of construction.

The Welcome Creek cabin was built in 1933 by George Purtilar and Hector Hoyt, seasonal Forest Service fire guards. The cost of the materials was $158.

The Green Fork cabin was constructed in 1935 by seasonal forest guards Harry Taylor and Grover Morton at a cost of $568.

The Pretty Prairie cabin was constructed in 1934 by Hector Hoyt and George Purtilar. The cost of materials was $694.

The Indian Point cabin was built in 1934 by Mac McIntyre and other seasonal employees. Material costs were $568.

The Cabin Creek cabin was built in 1934 by Paul Hazel and Harry Taylor, assisted by the summer fire guards. Cost of the materials was $793.

The first small **Benchmark** cabin was built by Ed Druckmiller, and the larger cabin was built in the mid-'20s.

The Willow Creek cabin was built in about 1924, and an older cabin before that, perhaps about 1908. The Basin Creek cabin was built in 1928, the Danaher cabin in 1932, the Gooseberry Park cabin in 1928, the Pentagon cabin in 1931 and the Pendant cabin was built in 1954.

In almost all cases the material was packed in by horse for each of these buildings.

Top: The Spotted Bear lookout in 1917. U.S. FOREST SERVICE PHOTO
Bottom: Three Forks Ranger Station in 1912. It was built in 1909. U.S. FOREST SERVICE PHOTO

NOTES ON INDIANS
by Rick and Susie Graetz

The Kootenai, Kalispell, Pend d'Oreille, Flathead and the Blackfeet Indian tribes roamed the Flathead River drainage. Their movements through and around this country followed their migration patterns determined by their search for bison and salmon, cambium and bitterroot. Deer and elk also constituted one of their major food resources as they were plentiful in these mountain regions.

The Indians on the west side of the Divide, and especially those in the Flathead Valley region, had to move eastward and through the present-day Bob Marshall in search of the bison. Some main trails existed as well as less-used paths. Many of these were utilized to avoid Blackfeet raiding parties that frequented the more heavily traveled routes.

In May of 1970, the Montana Statewide Archaeological Survey, Department of Anthropology, University of Montana, Missoula, contracted with the U.S. Forest Service to do an archaeological survey in areas adjacent to two rivers in the Bob Marshall. Artifacts were found: three of them on or near the Middle Fork of the Flathead, the rest on the South Fork of the Flathead River. Most sites showed evidence of short-term use while the Indians were passing through or hunting. Today, some of the identified places are used by horse packers. Many of the areas show evidence of stripping trees to get at their cambium layer, a food source. Sacagawea told Lewis and Clark of this practice. Cambium was gathered in May and June: the favorite trees were the ponderosa, lodgepole, white pine and aspen. After the outer bark was taken off, the cambium was removed in strips, rolled and wrapped in leaves to prevent drying and stored for use.

Forest Service trails today have been planned to follow the shortest routes between two points with a minimum of elevation change. In most cases, trails follow river bottoms through timber and must be maintained. The Indians traveled differently. Their paths conformed to natural routes and they often followed the open ridgelines and high river terraces or game trails.

The archaeological survey crew identified two major Indian routes across the Bob Marshall. They are easily visible, but now, only animals use them except where they come in contact with current Forest Service trails. The northern most path began in the northern Swan Valley near Echo Lake and went through Jewel Basin to the valley of the South Fork of the Flathead crossing in a area now inundated by Hungry Horse Lake. From there it traversed the Flathead Range to the Middle Fork of the Flathead and headed northeast to Marias Pass.

South of Swan Lake, another trail went up Soup Creek in the area of Inspiration Pass and down Bunker Creek to the South Fork of the Flathead. From there, it headed north to the confluence of the Spotted Bear River and the South Fork and then on up through the mountains of the southern end of the Flathead Range down Miner Creek to the Middle Fork of the Flathead and out through Lodgepole Creek over the Continental Divide into the valley of the Two Medicine River. The southernmost trail corresponds in many areas to a very popular trail from Holland Lake. This route climbed the Swan Crest from Holland Lake and then down Gordon Creek to the South Fork of the Flathead. It then pointed south to the area of Camp Creek and then northeast over Camp Creek Pass down through Pearl Basin and the West Fork of the South Fork of the Sun River on its way to the prairie.

These trails have been documented. However, other routes are evident, even today. If one abides by the theory that the Indian trails followed the natural terrain, then it is quite easy to find other routes across this wilderness complex. Many of the trails in existence today were either first used by Indians or the early-day trappers.

On almost every occasion when the archaeological survey crew left the river bottoms and moved onto higher ground, proof of early Indian use was commonplace. They concluded that the Indians found that the easiest and quickest means of travel on the high, open ridges. The researchers also believed that Indians used these areas because the game animals were there in the summer, it was cooler, and there were fewer bugs. Snowfields that existed well into the summer could have provided water in the absence of running creeks or streams.

Many of the camping sites were found in the large meadows where horses could be grazed. Evidence from personal testimony shows that the Kootenai had a camp at Spotted Bear where they grew tobacco and hunted.

A route reported to have been used by the Indians in modern times is Lions Creek Pass, near Swan Peak and down Palisades Creek to the valley of the South Fork of the Flathead. This was used by those coming from the Flathead Valley over Piper and Crow passes in the Mission Mountains.

Another documented Indian trail went up the Spotted Bear River to the Pentagon Mountain area to Dean Lake, down Basin Creek to Bowl Creek to the Middle Fork of the Flathead and then up Strawberry Creek to Gateway

Gorge, through the Big River Meadows over Gateway Pass and down the South Fork of Birch Creek. Another trail used on occasion went over Smith Creek Pass in the Swan Range and down Little Salmon Creek to the South Fork of the Flathead Valley. Also recorded was a route up Trail Creek and Morrell Creek. This was reached from the Jocko River Pass country of the Mission Mountains.

Pyramid Pass was a particularly popular route. In this case, the largest group of Indians camped in the Swan Valley and then sent smaller hunting parties over Pyramid Pass to Teepee Meadows and on to the Flathead River. Travois tracks are still evident in this area. The Teepee Park area is now called Leota Park. Hole In the Wall, also reached from Pyramid Pass, was another favorite campsite. A spot near here, on Kid Creek, was called Teeter-Totter Pass. The story goes that some Indian men were returning to camp and found the women and children playing on a roughly made teeter-totter. The Indians coming in over Pyramid Pass usually stayed for a couple of months from early September to late October. In the early 1930s, these hunting trips stopped. Some of the Indians died while in this region of the South Fork of the Flathead and were buried there.

Most of their camping activity was in the area now called Leota Park. From there they would hunt down toward the Big Prairie area or up into a region the Indians call Willow Creek, now the Danaher.

Big Salmon Lake, downstream from Big Prairie and just off the South Fork of the Flathead, was another highly used resting spot. The Indians caught fish and smoked them here.

On the east side of the Divide, the Blackfoot Indians used Camp Creek Pass coming up from the Sun River country and the Augusta region to get to the South Fork of the Flathead.

There is very little evidence that the Indians stayed in the Bob Marshall country year round. In the case of the Flathead drainage area, they tried to move out of the country by the third snow. An occasional tale tells of Indians not getting out before deep snow in the passes blocked their retreat, forcing them to stay in the river bottoms all winter. There is substantiation in the Big Prairie area, that some Indians were caught by early winter storms. The trees show signs of heavy peeling of cambium for survival purposes.

Believing the water had medicinal properties, Medicine Hot Springs at the confluence of the North and South Forks of the Sun River was a favored gathering place. Later, white settlers began using these hot pools and put walls around the springs. The water was about four feet deep and the temperature averaged about 86 degrees. Today, the original area has caved in. The waters have been diverted to a pool for use of a guest ranch now owned by the Klick family. This ranch is a small in-holding in the Bob Marshall Wilderness.

Indians also camped just downstream from Medicine Springs at Scattering Springs and in the Big George Gulch area along the Sun River. They called the Sun the Medicine River and Lewis and Clark named it as such on their first maps. Paul Hazel, who lived in the Sun River country for more than 50 years, speaks of finding arrowheads and artifacts in the Biggs Creek and Beartop area.

The Great North Trail was referred to by the Blackfeet Indians as the Travois Trail, and they followed it along the Rocky Mountain Front. Before their use, it was a route followed by migrating buffalo. Studies have shown that this trail perhaps extended well beyond the routes of the Indians and went as far north as Alaska and south into Mexico and farther.

In relation to the Rocky Mountain Front, the Great North Trail runs along the higher benches just below the Front. When the first cattlemen came to the Rocky Mountain Front region from the Judith Basin on their way to the Sun and Teton rivers, they found the trail easily recognizable by the travois tracks dug deeply in the sod. There are places where the marks are still plainly visible from a distance as grass filled depression or gullies running counter to the natural erosion pattern. In some places, the trail is signed with stone monuments put in place by Indians. Teepee rings may still be found at old camping spots along the way. More evidence of the trail may be seen near Green Timber Gulch, Wagner Basin and the Sun River Canyon, and again near Haystack Butte and the North Fork of the Dearborn River and Bean Lake. During the Blackfoot era, the trail had several routes. As it came out of the north in the Glacier country, it split in the vicinity of the Sun River with one branch going down the Missouri River to where Fort Benton is located and the other through Prickly Pear Canyon on its way to Helena.

Native Use of the Wilderness
by Charlie Shaw

This was Indian country before the arrival of the white man. Blackfeet Indian country was to the east of the Front and Flathead Indian country extended from that valley to the west. These two tribes could never be considered very friendly or congenial toward each other and often met in pitched battles in this mountainous country. The Blackfeet had an abundance of buffalo to supply their wants, while there were no buffalo west of the Continental Divide, north of the state of Utah. The Flatheads crossed the mountains to secure their buffalo. The Blackfeet entered the mountains to their west to fish the mountain streams.

There are brief reports of major battles between these two tribes. David Thompson, one of the earliest white fur traders in the area (about 1811), mentions one battle that took place near the mouth of Morrison Creek on the Middle Fork of the Flathead River. In this skirmish the Flatheads, supposedly, lost heavily. A major battle took place in the 1840s in what is now the Bob Marshall Wilderness. In the vicinity of Camp Creek, above Big Prairie, on the South Fork of the Flathead River. The Flatheads had been to the prairie east of Augusta on a buffalo hunt and were returning with their meat and a few extra ponies. They were camped near Basin Creek. Scouts had been left behind to report on any activity or to ascertain if they were being followed by the Blackfeet. Soon, one of the scouts charged into the encampment to announce that a large number of hostile Blackfeet were approaching the Divide from the east.

The Flathead broke camp immediately. Women and children moved the camp down The South Fork to the open meadows near the present site of the Big Prairie Ranger Station. The warriors and braves moved back up the creek, stationed themselves in strategic positions on either side of the canyon, and awaited their foe.

When the Blackfeet arrived, on a signal from their chief, the Flatheads opened fire from ambush. Taken by complete surprise, the Blackfeet were almost annihilated. A few Blackfeet raced back over the Divide in panic. Ranger J.R Hutchinson told me this story in 1934, while we were on a snowshoe trip on game studies in this area.

Camp Creek seems to have been a favorite camping site for the Flathead Indians. There were several prominent tepee rings on this flat Many Indian artifacts have been found in this vicinity.

There are Indian paintings at several locations just outside the Bob Marshall. Paintings at the junction of the North and South Forks of the Sun River appear to depict a symbol representing the Sun. Perhaps this is how the river got its name.

A cave at the base of Union Peak, just southwest of the present Schafer Station, has the appearance of having been inhabited — smoky ceiling at the entrance. There is no record of this cave having been studied by archaeologists. The last time I was there (1944), the entrance was nearly closed by talus.

Indians used many different routes to the buffalo country on the prairies. One main route was retraced and posted in 1932 by Supervisor Kenneth Wolfe. This route is over Inspiration Pass from Goat Creek, from the Swan Valley, down Bunker Creek to Meadow Creek, down the South Fork, to the mouth of the Spotted Bear River, up the Spotted Bear and over Gunsight Pass, down Minor Creek, up Morrison, Lodgepole, over the Divide east of Big Lodge Mountain, down the Badger to the plains south of East Glacier. The route is still marked by a wooden sign near the mouth of Morrison Creek. There is also evidence today of the old Indian trail from the Flathead Valley over the Swan Divide; it crosses just south of Mount Aeneas, near Birch Lake.

CHARLIE SHAW worked on Flathead Forest Ranger Districts for 31 years starting in 1922. He retired in 1964 while at the Northern Region Headquarters in Missoula.

FIRE IN THE BOB
by Rick and Susie Graetz

Like any other mountain forested area, the Bob Marshall country has seen its share of major fires. Large areas of burn scars are still very much in evidence today. Of particular note is the country along the southern half of the Chinese Wall, almost down to Moose Creek and all the way across to the White River. This fire occurred in 1910, the year of the greatest fires in history in the northern Rocky Mountains. In the year of 1910, fires were burning all over the Bob Marshall Wilderness. The White River fire jumped the divide and burned down into the Sun River drainages as well as along the Chinese Wall. It has been estimated that this fire burned upwards of 75,000 to 100,000 acres. The same year, a much larger fire between 120,000 to 150,000 acres burned in the Schafer Meadows area.

Like any other mountain forested area, the Bob Marshall country has seen its share of major fires. Large areas of burn scars are still very much in evidence today. Of particular note is the country along the southern half of the Chinese Wall, almost down to Moose Creek and all the way across to the White River. This fire occurred in 1910, the year of the greatest fires in history in the northern Rocky Mountains. In the year of 1910, fires were burning all over the Bob Marshall Wilderness. The White River fire jumped the divide and burned down into the Sun River drainages as well as along the Chinese Wall. It has been estimated that this fire burned upwards of 75,000 to 100,000 acres. The same year, a much larger fire between 120,000 to 150,000 acres burned in the Schafer Meadows area.

Besides 1910, other major fire years in the Bob Marshall were 1889, 1903, 1926, 1929 and 1940. Since then however, acreage burned has subsided. The manning of lookouts, the development of the smoke jumper program, the use of fire retardants and better access to the back country have minimized these burns. And public attitude was fires should be suppressed, not a very good idea in all cases.

Then in the incredibly dry late spring and summer of 1988, enormous fires blew up throughout the Northern Rockies including the 245,000 acre Canyon Creek Fire in southern Bob Marshall country. In the North Fork of the Sun drainage the Gates Park Fire blackened 55,000 acres.

In 2000, the Bunyan Point Fire charred 1000 acres in the Scapegoat and that same summer, The McDonald I fire (west of Sun River Pass) involved only one tree that was hit by lightening and it went out, but then a subsequent strike started the larger 4,500 acre MacDonald II Fire. The second conflagration crossed into the north end of the 1988 Gates Park fire creating a desirable situation termed reoccurrence of fire. This cleans up a previously burned

The 1988 Canyon Creek fire blows up. RICK AND SUSIE GRAETZ

142

Steve Copenhaven in Limestone Pass — 1988 Canyon Creek fire in the distance. RICK AND SUSIE GRAETZ

area by consuming fuel and burns a sizeable number of the new lodgepole pine before they are mature enough for seeds to be released. This new growth after the first fire is usually dense. The reburn allows for a thinning process and creates age diversification.

Fire struck again in 2001 with the 8,500 acre Biggs Flat fire, between Gates Park and Gibson Lake. It reburned 93% of the Gates Park Fire.

The Salmon Complex fire in 2003 grew to 88,000 acres touching mountain sides west of the South Fork of the Flathead River and the Big Salmon Lake area.

We can't and shouldn't eliminate fires as they are part of the natural system. But we as a public have spent 90 years creating unnatural conditions by trying to eradicate them. Owing to this mind-set, when fire comes, often times it is catastrophic. Natural caused fires need to be promoted and should be managed rather than suppressed to reduce the risk of ruinous fires in the future.

The Canyon Creek Fire of 1988 is an example. It spread well beyond the wilderness because there was so much fuel from years of fighting fire.

In recent years the Forest Service has allowed fires to burn such as the Biggs Flat burn calling it a Wildland Fire Use Area. A visit to the Biggs Flat Country or Gates Parks show the value of these fires, especially the reoccurring ones. Wildlife habitat is improved, views are opened up and in general the landscape is better off. It is important to know the USFS has plans in place for each fire allowed to run so they know when suppressive work is necessary. If the burn stays in the wilderness it is allowed to follow its natural inclinations. The Biggs and Gates fires had natural barriers on the east by way of the steep rocky crags of the Rocky Mountain Front.

Because of short growing seasons, thin soils, lack of seed and moisture, tree growth in some burned-over areas, especially in the high country, has been slow. Grass and low lying vegetation comes back rapidly. On the better sites, especially in the wetter areas, west of the Continental Divide and in the northern reaches of the wilderness, recovery is much faster.

In October 2003, the Rocky Mountain Ranger District started a fire called the South Fork of the Sun Prescribed fire in the Scapegoat. This to help remove fuel and to prevent bigger fires in the future. It is planned for a perimeter of 16,000 acres where fire can exist without having to take action to extinguish it. Plans however call for only injecting 10,000 acres and then doing that in blocks or stages over a five year period if it takes that long. In the Fall of 2003, 4,287 acres burned before it went out with fall snows. Stage II is planned for Fall 2004 and calls for only 1,048 acres. If conditions allow though both blocks II and III (11.166 acres) will burn and the project will be completed.

It is interesting to note that since 1939, almost all of the east side of the Bob Marshall country had burned at one time or another.

NAMES OF THE BOB MARSHALL

Alice Creek named for Alice Cox who died at an early age; family homesteaded in the area.

Arsenic Mountain and Creek named by early-day settlers because of odor of the creek. And the water never freezes.

Baptiste Creek and Mountain are named for Felix Baptiste; some knew him as Baptiste Zeroyal. He was an early-day trapper and was instrumental in naming Spotted Bear. He is buried near his cabin on Hoke Creek. Felix Creek is also named for Baptiste.

Bartlett Creek and Mountain are named for a Forest Service employee.

Belton is named for James Belton, early trapper.

Benchmark named by original surveyors in the early '20s for the section-line benchmarks in the immediate area. Benchmark Creek — from U.S. Geological Survey benchmark established in 1900 on the north bank of the creek.

Big Bull Creek and Mountain are named for a trail foreman of 1914.

Big George Gulch named for early homesteader, trapper, and ladies' man, Big George Mathews.

Biggs Creek named after Charles Biggs who in about 1866 cut railroad ties along the North Fork Sun River.

Bloody Hill named for an incident involving a Forest Service mule that bucked off a pack, including a cross cut saw. The mule became entangled in the saw and was badly cut up. Another story about the origin of this name involves a battle between two tribes. The Blackfeet nearly wiped out a Flathead hunting party at this site. However, there is no historical evidence of the fight.

Bruce Creek is named for Flathead National Forest Supervisor Donald Bruce (1914–915). When Bruce was married, a large branch of this creek was named Addition Creek. When the Bruces' first child was born, a large fork of Addition Creek was named Little Creek.

Bum Shot Mountain named for a local hunting outfit. Two members of the party ran into small herd of elk and emptied their rifles without drawing blood.

Bunker Creek named for Page S. Bunker, Flathead National Forest Supervisor, 1905–1913.

Calbick Creek is named for Allen Calbick, early ranger.

Clack Creek is named for Jack Clack, early Assistant Supervisor of the Flathead.

Cooney Creek and Mountain named for an outlaw.

Coram is named for William Coram, early-day Kalispell timberman.

Creeks in the Lower South Fork — Mazie, Anna, Pearl, Goldie, Emma, Flossie, Elya, Maggie, Mamie, Doris and others - were named for the girls the U.S.G.S. men met in town.

Danaher Creek and Mountain are named for Thomas Danaher, early Ranger who homesteaded here in 1898. His homestead was in what is now the Bob Marshall Wilderness.

Danaher River and Meadows also named for Thomas Danaher, homesteader; some old horse drawn h ay equipment remains in Danaher meadow.

Dean Ridge, Creek and Lake are named for Richard Dean, early Ranger in the area (1913–1914).

Dearborn River *"This handsome bold and clear stream we named in honor of the Secretary of War calling it the Dearborn's river."* Capt. Meriwether Lewis, July 18, 1805.

Dirty Face Creek is named for *"Dirty Face"* McDonald, early trapper and prospector.

Flathead River named for a group of Salish-speaking Indians living in the area. The group was called Flathead by other local Indian groups, in the belief that Flatheads pressed the heads of their young to flatten them. The Flatheads say the belief is false.

Gates Park named after homesteader named Cates. The name was misspelled.

Gibson Reservoir named for Paris Gibson, founder of Great Falls.

Gordon Creek and Doctor Lake are named for Dr. Gordon, who established the Gordon Ranch near Holland Lake.

Great Bear Creek and Mountain were named by Senator Penrose of Pennsylvania.

Great Northern Mountain named for Great Northern Railroad.

Grimsley Creek and Grimsley Park are named for *"Chick"* Grimsley, early-day trapper and guide. Grimsley came from Texas with a trail herd as a boy and located near the Blackfoot Indian Agency. He came into the Middle Fork in 1896.

Hahn Creek misspelled from the name of Frank D. Haun, an early day forester.

Hahn Peak named for Tom Hahn, who trapped in the area in 1908.

Hannan Gulch Jim Hannan a local homesteader who operated a station for horse thieves on the Oregon Trail, also liked to eat his neighbors' beef steak. Local cattlemen left a hangman's noose on a tree near Hannan's house (in what is now Hannan's Gulch) and put several bullet holes in his front door. After that, Hannan was never seen in the area again. The bullet holes were still in the door when the cabin became a Ranger Station.

Hart Creek and Basin are named for Evert Hart, Forest Service employee who built the Limestone and Black Bear cabins in 1925.

Headquarters Pass and Creek The creek originally was named Tie Hacker Creek because of many cabins built by tie hackers (railroad tie cutters) in the area. It later became a headquarters for tie hackers, hence the name headquarters.

Hoke Creek is named for Ranger Ellis B. Hoke.

Holbrook Creek and Mountain are named for Ranger Fred Holbrook. A Mormon, Holbrook was raised by Brigham Young's favorite wife, Amelia.

Holland Lake named for the first settler, B.B. Holland.

Hungry Horse got its name because two horses became lost in the area and nearly starved.

Koessler Lake is named after Doctor Koessler.

Logan Creek is named for Sidney M. Logan, who worked mining claims in this area.

Marshall Creek is named for a trapper. He died about 1918.

Monture Creek named for George Montour, a half-breed who was killed by Indians near the mouth of the North Fork of the Blackfoot River.

Morrell Creek named after Fred Morrell, early-day ranger.

Mortimer Gulch named for Johnnie Mortimer, a recluse homesteader and confirmed bachelor.

Moser Mountain named after early-day Forest Supervisor headquartered at Ovando.

Mt. Bradley and Bradley Creek are named for Richard Bradley, early-day Forest Ranger in the area.

Mt. Drewyer phonetic spelling honoring George Drouillard, an interpreter and hunter for the Lewis and Clark expedition.

Mt. Field misspelled from the name of Joseph and Reuben Fields, brothers from Kentucky shown on the Lewis and Clark Expedition roll.

Mt. Forester is named for W.J. Forester, member of a U.S.G.S. crew of 1914.

Mt. Frazier named after Robert Frazier, member of the Lewis and Clark expedition.

Mt. Furlong is named for James Furlong, early trapper and prospector. He worked for the Great Northern from 1900 to 1924.

Mount Liebig is named for Frank Liebig who trained in Germany as a forester and came to the Flathead area at the turn of the century. His first Ranger District assignment was in 1901 in what is now Glacier National Park.

Mount Lockhart named for a former Lewis and Clark National Forest Supervisor, killed by a horse at the old cabin at the Base of Mount Lockhart.

Mt. Patrick Gass after Patrick Gass, a member of Lewis and Clark Expedition.

Mt. Werner named after Willard Werner a member of the Lewis and Clark expedition.

Mount Wright Capt. Wright was in charge of tie and wood cutting operations for the government at the head of Teton River in 1908.

Murphy Flats between Holbrook and Salmon Forks, is named for Joe Murphy, an outfitter from Ovando. He and his family have used this area as a campsite since 1919.

Neil Creek near Reclamation Flats was named after Bruce Neal.

Phil Creek named for Phillip Clack, former Ranger, and brother of former Assistant Supervisor Jack Clack.

Renshaw Mountain Renshaw was an early-day tie hacker.

Rogers Pass named for Milwaukee railroad surveyor who surveyed the area.

Scapegoat Mountain USGS surveyor (Chapman), working in the area in 1897–1900, gave the peak the name Scapegoat after he had difficulty surveying the area.

Scarface Mountain named for a Piegan Indian God.

Schafer Meadows and Creek are named for William Schafer, a trapper. His headquarters cabin was at Schafer Meadow. He was found dead in his cabin in 1908. Circumstances indicated he had been robbed. He was buried on Morrison Creek near the mouth of Lodgepole Creek.

Shaw Creek and Mountain are named for Ezra Shaw, early-day ranger at Seeley Lake.

Shields Creek and Mountain are named for Thomas Shields, Great Northern Railroad telegraph operator and Essex postmaster. **Marion Lake** is named for his daughter, and Almeda Lake, for his wife.

Slippery Bill Mountain and Morrison Creek are named for William H. Morrison, early-day trapper and forest ranger. He had squatter's rights on 160 acres at Summit, where he lived by his wits until he died in Kalispell in March 1932.

Sock Lake A trail and fire crew were camped at the head of Red Shale Creek while working on a fire on Moonlight Peak in the '20s. They visited the lake to *"mop up"* and found socks hanging in the trees, thus the name.

Spotted Bear is one of the oldest known names in the Flathead National Forest. This name has been attached to a river, a mountain, and a Forest Service Ranger Station in the South Fork area. The story of how this name originated was related to Charlie Shaw by the late Harry Wilson, one of the more rugged individuals who trapped and prospected for a living in this country. It was in the winter of 1933–34. Wilson invited Ranger Albert Campbell and Shaw to spend the night in Wilson's cabin on Sullivan Creek. They were making a big-game study in the area. During the evening, Wilson explained that back in about 1861, two prosperous California miners were looking for a guide to pack them through the mountains to the east side of the Continental Divide. Inquiring at the Hudson Bay Trading Post at Salish for a good guide, they were referred to Baptiste Zeroyal, better known as Felix Baptiste or just Baptiste. Few men in those days were more familiar with this wilderness area than Baptiste. Because the Blackfeet Indians were more or less perpetually on the warpath at that time, Baptiste decided the best route to travel was up the South Fork and Spotted Bear Rivers and down Sun River. One day on the journey, while camped near the mouth of the Spotted Bear River, they saw a black bear with an unusual amount of white on its breast and underside. Thus, the name Spotted Bear was created.

Spotted Eagle Mountain named for one of the Blackfeet Indian chiefs who signed 1895 treaty that ceded the area to the Government.

Sullivan Creek is named for a former Spotted Bear District Ranger, John Sullivan.

Swan Range and River named for the large number of trumpeter swans in the area.

Two Medicine River named by Blackfeet Indians. They believed the high mountains on the eastern edge of Glacier Park had spiritual powers. The two forks of the Two Medicine River drain this area, thus the name Two Medicine or Big Medicine.

Waldbillig Mountain near the head of Gordon Creek on the Big Prairie District, is named for a Forest Service employee and game warden. About 1906, he was killed while attempting to arrest a group of Flathead Indians caught violating game laws in the Pendant Creek area. Another game warden by the name of Morgan from Ovando came in and packed out the body. The Indians fled. No one was ever convicted for this murder.

Wall Creek is named for Chet Wall, Forest Service employee.

White River is named for Steward Edward White, famous author.

Youngs Creek named after Charles *"Kid"* Young who trapped and worked for the Forest Service at the turn of the the century.

South Fork of the Flathead.   U.S. FOREST SERVICE PHOTO

SHOULDERS TO THE WHEEL
by Jim Posewitz

The spirits of many dwell in this wild land. They haunt the deep shadows of the spruce thickets. Their souls sing across barren ridges and murmur among the pines. Their ashes mingle silently in the duff of the forest floor. These are the memories and mortal substance of people who gave of themselves and sustained the life of one of America's noblest concepts — the preservation of wilderness.

Men are bonded to the earth. The American farmer turning furrow after endless furrow loves his *"place,"* enduring anything to keep it. Cowmen appreciate grass, and swell with pride over the spread of their prairie. Wild land, too, is loved — passionately. It is a love that drives conservationists from every stratum of American society to gather or go singly on crusades of preservation. It has been so in the Bob Marshall country for generations. Always there have been people who cared enough to stand and defend this place. Archaeologists tell us modern man has roamed this planet since about 35,000BC. Within the last century, the human concept of preserving a small part of what we were given emerged. This idea grew to reality in perhaps the only nation where free men had a fighting chance to make it happen. In making preservation happen, it was seldom, if ever, a matter of men joining a popular cause. Rather, it seemed to be someone fighting for an ideal that challenged the momentum of exploitative forces of awesome dimension. In a pioneering nation, wilderness was to be conquered. At first, only a few chose to challenge that conventional wisdom.

Today, the beginnings of the preservation movement — the effort to stop the total conquest — are still in sight. The tracks laid down by the founding fathers are still etched plainly in the sand.

Many have trod these tortuous courses. It is not the purpose of this chapter to print the roster of all who answered when the land lay vulnerable and threatened. The purpose is only to touch on a few who declared: this land shall not perish, shall not fade, this land shall remain as God created it and as free men will it to remain.

In time, many chronicles will add to the history and the truth of the preservation of the Bob Marshall country. The list of heroes in the struggle will grow; time will eventually call up all the right names. Should the recorders of events fail and leave some deed or individual without proper notice, there is the greater comfort in knowing the land will not forget. It will fondly stand in remembrance of each and every contribution, its future a total reflection of some person's deed.

Three major battles and a hundred skirmishes have molded the Bob. The centerpiece was born in the minds of men who loved just plain wilderness and simultaneously, in the hearts of people striving to protect and restore the wildlife of the Northern Rockies.

Any discussion of those who held the land for us must start with the man, Bob Marshall. A Forest Service professional, he was a tireless and successful advocate for wild land within his agency. It was a time when such advocacy was tolerated and successful. The agency viewed itself as protector of the forest first and exploitative uses second. Sadly, it was an attitude that would change before the Lincoln-Scapegoat was added to the Bob Marshall country.

In the late 1920s, Bob Marshall was assistant silveiculturist at the Forest Service's Northern Rocky Mountain Forest and Range Experiment Station in Missoula. His trips into the backcountry became legend and he tirelessly explored the deep wilderness that in time would bear his name.

In 1929, the USFS established regulations that provided for protection of areas as *"primitive"* — they were known as the *"L"* regulations. Later, a new classification, the *"U"*, as designed and three areas — the upper Sun River, Pentagon and upper South Fork of the Flathead were parts of this classification. By 1934, Marshall was in Washington, D.C. arguing, pleading and insisting on the preservation of wilderness within the system of forest management.

That same year, two men profoundly interested in wild-land preservation were in the Sun River country studying the recovery of the area's elk herd. Sitting up late one night in a cabin on Cabin Creek up the Sun River's North Fork, they talked of the need for wilderness to secure both land and elk. These two, Bob Cooney, then with the USFS and assigned to the Sun River elk herd and his mentor, Dr. Olas Murie, one of the founding fathers of the Wilderness Society then working for the U. S. Fish and Wildlife Service out of Jackson Hole, Wyoming, quietly put their shoulders to the wheel and helped make it roll. Marshall continued to advocate the principle of wilderness nationwide, and Cooney carried on in Montana emphasizing the preservation of wildlife by protecting land. It was an agenda internal to government agencies, and it led to success.

Bob Marshall died in 1939, and in 1940, the three primitive areas were united into one Forest Service-classified wilderness and named in his honor. Cooney went to work for the Montana Fish and Game Department and continued pulling for wilderness and wildlife until his retirement and beyond — his shoulder still to the wheel.

In the 1940s, recovery of the area's wildlife, particularly elk, provided the first crisis and initiated an era of broad public involvement in wildland/wildlife preservation. The growing elk herd was causing friction with private landowners along the Rocky Mountain Front. Cooney and Bruce Neal, a true mountain-man, were trying to hold the elk back in the mountains, away from private ground. Recognizing that the elk needed a foothills winter range, they turned to Montana's people. The man they found was Tom Messelt, a Great Falls businessman, sportsman and first secretary of the Montana Wildlife Federation. Messelt understood peace had to be declared between hunters and ranchers if the problem were to be solved.

Messelt organized the Sun River Conservation Council, a was a citizen's group including Al Riegel and Jess Gleason representing, along with Messelt, sportsmen from Helena, Choteau and the Great Falls. Livestock interests were voiced by Charles Willard, Carl Malone and Les Barrett. The break came late in 1947, when an elderly rancher named Brucegard put his place up for sale. The adjoining Wortheimer ranch came up for sale at the same time, and together they would make an ideal winter elk range. The Fish and Game Department needed to put up a $10,000 down payment, and they had but a few hours to do it in or lose it to another buyer. Even in 1947, government couldn't move fast enough; the future hung by a thread.

Archie O'Claire, director of the Fish and Game Department, turned to the Sun River Conservation Council — in a magnanimous move, Messelt, the sportsman, and Malone, the Choteau rancher, made the down payment. Bruce Neal, who lived with the elk all those long winters herding them back into the mountains, was installed as first game-range manager; he could now welcome the Sun River herd to the first real winter home of their own since white men settled the Rocky Mountain Front. Another chapter in rebuilding the Bob Marshall country was completed, and perhaps for the first time, its authors were hunters, ranchers and a host of Montana people who simply cared. A new blueprint was clearly emerging in the history of this land. It was a pattern of public support for the preservation of cherished values, wild places and animals living free.

In the late 1920s, a small storage reservoir, Gibson Dam, and a diversion dam downstream on the Sun River were built in Sun River Canyon. Ironically, the storage dam blocked the primitive access to upper Sun River and, for all practical purposes, livestock grazing and cutting for railroad ties in the backcountry.

By 1950, the Bureau of Reclamation advanced plans for another dam and development that would take more land, block elk migration routes, good bighorn sheep winter ranges and elk calving areas. The proposal was known as Upper Sun Butte Dam to be located between Sun Butte and Sheep Reef. Sportsmen, dude ranchers, outfitters, the Montana Fish and Game Department and others rose in unison against the proposal. The threat quickly subsided, but only momentarily.

In 1953, the first in a series of floods swept the country, followed by more in 1964 and 1975. The '53 flood brought the Bureau of Reclamation out in full force. Two more even larger dams were now on the agenda. One, Lower Sun Butte at the confluence of the North and South Fork of the Sun River, the other, a plant at the mouth of Sun River Canyon. Another skirmish was on.

About this same time in 1958, the Montana Wilderness Association was formed with Dr. John Montagne and Ken and Florence Baldwin, all of Bozeman, as leading advocates for protecting Sun River Canyon and the wilderness beyond. The Montana Wildlife Federation was the dominant sportsman's group and Don Aldrich of Missoula was its spokesman. The Cascade County Sportsmen's Association, often at odds with other groups over elk management, joined the alliance to save Sun River Canyon, and the Bureau of Reclamation soon retreated to await the next flood.

Mrs. Frances Allen, owner of the K-L dude ranch at the head of Gibson reservoir, was a most eloquent spokesperson during the dam battles. On her death, her estate created the Allen Foundation, which to this day makes contributions to the preservation of the Sun River Canyon and the wildlife of her beloved landscape.

In 1964, another flood gave the Bureau of Reclamation new life, but again the people united against them; the conservationists remained clearly dominant The Wilderness Act was passed by the Congress, the Bob Marshall was at that point formally wilderness, and the dam-building threats passed into history. About this time, in the country to the north, the same problems plagued the Middle Fork of the Flathead and a whole new conservation group evolved there to defend the wild lands and waters of that area; its leaders, Dr. Loren Kreck of Columbia Falls. Dr. John Craighead, the noted grizzly bear expert who also developed a wild-rivers concept, and others formed a solid nucleus of leadership that eventually grew into a constituency for the Great Bear Wilderness.

The meeting to form the organization called the Citizens for the Great Bear Wilderness. Photo taken in the parking lot of Trixie's Saloon at Ovando, Montana. Meeting date March 12, 1977. DALE BURKE

With the subsidence of the dam builders' threat, it was clear that the core of the country, the Bob Marshall Wilderness, was solid. The people now looked to extending wilderness protection to adjacent wild lands becoming vulnerable to surging product demands and a changing Forest Service philosophy.

The first blatant evidence of a changing attitude that aroused conservationists occurred in the Bunker Creek drainage. Bunker Creek, a tributary of the South Fork of the Flathead, was well known to Kalispell sportsmen. It was elk, goat and grizzly country. The streams were important for bull trout and west slope cutthroat trout. It was also timber country and the Forest Service was after timber. Leaders emerged to contest the federal commodity merchants. It was a bitter contest, fought before any environmental laws were enacted and fought before the public was guaranteed access to federal decision-making. It was a tough time, but state employment agency workers Clif Merritt and Dallas Eklund, who surfaced as the leaders, were also tough. Bob Sikes and Forrest Rockwood, both Kalispell attorneys, joined the fray. They were people whose names would continue to arise as issue after issue was faced in and around the Bob Marshall country. Bunker Creek fell to the bulldozer and chainsaw. Though they lost this battle, conservationists would gather to fight another day, Bunker Creek would not easily be forgotten.

First on the people's agenda was the Lincoln backcountry, an area long considered a wilderness land and managed as a wilderness by the Forest Service, but without formal recognition as wilderness by Congress. In 1947, the Forest Service conducted *"show me"* trips into the country to convince influential citizens of the need for preservation. A Forest Service employee, Donald Roos, later said his instructions were to *"sell these men on the beauty and solitude of the back country, to show them a part of the country and solitude of the back country, to show them a part of the country that was as God made it; unspoiled, quiet."* That attitude changed in 1968 when the Forest Service revealed plans to develop the Lincoln backcountry. Montana's people responded with an overwhelming protest and were ultimately successful. The Scapegoat Wilderness was enacted into law in 1972, and adjoined the Bob Marshall. That story in depth, appears elsewhere in this book.

Peace was fleeting. Now, between the Bob Marshall and Glacier National Park, a wild, unprotected landscape and river would soon become a hotly contested terrain. The Middle Fork of the Flathead, had seen skirmishes before. In the 1950s, the federal engineers proposed a dam known as Spruce Park for the Middle Fork. Local conservationists, led by Dallas Eklund, Leland Schoonover, and Clif Merritt, as well as Archie O'Claire and Bob Cooney of the Fish and Game Department, never let it get off the ground.

The move fore preservation of the Middle Fork and a vast portion of its watershed, the Great Bear, was escalating into an intense and ultimately bitter struggle. The river was designated for study when Congress passed the National Wild and Scenic Rivers Act in 1969. The Forest Service conducted the mandated study, and with overwhelming public support, recommended the upper Middle Fork be *"wild"* — the most stringent classification option open to them. Before the end of 1976, Congress agreed, and a major victory was achieved. Key players in the campaign were Dr. John Craighead, who pioneered the wild and scenic river concept; Dale Burk, outdoor writer and reporter for the dominant newspaper in western Montana, the Missoulian; Dr. Loren Kreck of Columbia Falls, and Bigfork residents Rick Trembath and Frank Noise.

The victory celebration was short-lived, for the conservationists were well aware of the fact that the Wild and Scenic Rivers Act gave little, if any, protection to the watershed that gives birth to the quality of wild waters. They knew full well that the bigger battle for the uplands, the Great Bear Wilderness, lay ahead. The Great Bear Wilderness proposal was not new. The obvious wild-land qualities caused a sportsmen's group in Kalispell to advocate its addition to the Bob Marshall in the mid-1950s. The Forest Service turned that request down. For the moment, land management in the Middle Fork slipped into limbo.

With conclusion of the Lincoln-Scapegoat classification battle to the south, it was obvious that the Forest Service would be adverse to designating future land as wilderness. Their ill-conceived management plan for Lincoln's backcountry had served only to galvanize a level of public support for wilderness that overwhelmingly carried the issue. Having learned from the failure of their relatively *"up-front"* approach, their new strategy was evident when it came time to engage the issue of the Great Bear.

The veterans of the battle to protect the river, working with a number of conservation groups, succeeded in getting a state legislative resolution passed asking that the area be protected. Ignoring, or at least taking no visible heed of the resolution, the Forest Service simply started selling trees, building roads and making plans to generally level the forests in the drainage. It was before the National Environmental Policy Act existed, and public disclosure was primarily by leaks and dogged, hard-nosed snooping by those determined to pry off the lid and see just what was in store for the public land. Reporter Burk was masterful in this regard and as a result, public response once again reached a new pinnacle.

Just how Burk became involved is a classic tale that demonstrates how a chain reaction among people who care can lead to success. An outfitter named Smoke Elser thought what the country needed was publicity and packed Lloyd Shermer, publisher of the Lee Newspaper group in Montana, into the Great Bear. Shermer was so impressed that he called Burk from the first telephone he could find and insisted, *"I want you in here next week to do a story about this, to save the Middle Fork of the Flathead."* And so that's how Burk found himself working as a hand in Smoke Elser's outfit. He helped pack a group of people — some of whom were interested in the area's timber resources — into the backcountry. It had been set up for the local Forest Supervisor to ride in and layout his development plans to these folks. The night the forester spoke, Burk had his story, the people had the truth, and the Great Bear had an advocate.

A core of conservationists recruited on Bunker Creek, seasoned on the river classification issue, and now informed by Burk, soon enlisted an aggressive constituency that rallied to the Great Bear. A representative group of the rapidly swelling ranks of people willing to make a commitment for wild-land preservation met at Trixie's Bar in Ovando. The group included: Tom Horobik, Bill Cunningham, Loren Kreck Smoke Elser, Chris Roholt, Gene Sentz, Arlo Skari, Carly McCawiey, Don Marble, Jean Warren, Beth Williams, Bob Anderson, Dallas Eklund, Doris Milner, Jim Posewitz, Bill Bishop, Rick Trembath, Rod Barkley, Dale Burk, and Bonnle Horobik, Phil Tawney, and others.

The real giant of the Great Bear campaign was without doubt Montana's U. S. Senator Lee Metcalf. Metcalf's recruitment to the cause of the Great Bear was quite casual. In the final days of the Lincoln-Scapegoat classification process, Cecil Garland and Dale Burk were in Washington, D.C. to testify on the legislation. Talking with Garland on the possibility of taking on the Great Bear next, Burk was told. *"You'll never get the Great Bear, it's the wrong wilderness at the wrong time."* Undissuaded, Burk walked to the Senate office building and knocked on Lee Metcalf's door. After interviewing the Senator on another matter, Burk asked, *"I would like you to carry a cause on the Great Bear Wilderness."* Burk remembers the Senator's response this way: *"He said 'I'll do it.' Never anything other than that, just 'I'll do it.'"* Senator Metcalf seized the reins and it was only a matter of time before the Forest Service's rush to alter and compromise the land was halted and wilderness classification was achieved for the Great Bear in 1978.

Trial riders along the Chinese Wall in what was then the Sun River Primitive Area. Photo taken in 1935.   K.D. SWAN/U.S. FOREST SERVICE

Perhaps it is in the nature of the land; perhaps it is in the nature of man; perhaps it is simply that this place is such a treasure, it must be fought for to be appreciated. Another enemy of the wilderness was about to rear its ugly head. Oil, gas, energy — the irresistible force of our industrialized culture — could not wait to test its strength against the wild country and its band of advocates. Propelled by a series of energy *"crises"* and encouraged by the rhetoric of the Secretary of the Interior James Watt, the energy industry wanted access to the wilderness. First were seismic applications and lease applications to be debated and struggled over. Again, and now in a predictable pattern, the Montana conservationists rushed to the barricades. Organizations popped up overnight, coalitions developed — most important, leaders came to the front. Missoula veterinarian Jim Brogger of the Backcountry Horsemen led the specifically created Bob Marshall Alliance in the defense of the Bob Marshall country. People like Bill Cunningham of Helena, Arnold Bolle of Missoula, and Bill Bishop of Polson, were seasoned and sophisticated advocates from the Montana Wilderness Association. Smoke Elser, Chuck Blixrud, and Max Barker securely anchored the outfitters in the battle. Bud Moore, retired forester of Swan Lake, and Bob Cooney brought the wisdom, reason and credibility earned over almost a half century of experience; George Engler, the savvy of a sensitive retired forester who knew how the system worked added still another dimension. These people and many other veterans provided the fuel for the battle and the new legions added the fire. New names and faces quickly lined up for counting — Hank Fischer of Missoula; Ed Madej, Rosemary Rowe of Helena; Joan Montagne of Bozeman, and many more.

The first salvo was a request for a seismic permit and when the dust settled, Tom Coston, regional forester, denied the application. Still, seismic helicopters swarmed like angry bees around the wilderness boundary and applications for leasing within the three wilderness areas grew to cover virtually the entire land mass. While the debate raged in Montana, the issue quickly escalated to Washington, D.C. and became a test of strength and determination between Congress and Interior Secretary Watt. The wilderness was well represented by Montana's Western District Congressman Pat Williams, who proved to be nothing short of an angry silvertip when it came to the Bob Marshall and its defense. He led with effective withdrawal resolutions, amendments and direct legislative action — always one valuable step ahead of those who would seize an advantage and press a claim on the wilderness. With every plaintive cry that we must develop every conceivable energy resource, his response was simple,

From the Pearl Basin area looking toward the peaks of the Flathead Alps in 1937. U.S. FOREST SERVICE PHOTO

swift, certain and effective. *"No. Not here you don't."* and he made it stick. In less than a year, Pat Williams made a mark whose impact is sure to last for generations.

There were others, people like Les Pengelly — wildlife professor, Eldon and Liz Smith — educators and advocates, always close to every issue, preparing testimony, training and helping new advocates. The important thing is, there was always and continues to be someone to step in and fight for the wilderness.

JIM POSEWITZ of Helena has a Master's Degree in Fish and Wildlife Management from Montana State University and for more than 32 years worked with the Montana Department of Fish, Wildlife and Parks. He has directed much of his energy towards preservation of wildlands and rivers and has received many recognitions for his professional activity and work with citizens organizations. Today he is head of the Orion the Hunter's Institute as well as several other public interest organizations.

WILDERNESS
by A.B. Guthrie, Jr.

Packhorse trains travel the mountain wilderness, as do explorers on foot. Nothing mechanized is allowed, including bikes and chainsaws. The lift of peak, the depth of streambed, the sparkle of live water and, almost hidden in this great jumble of earth, the blue sapphire of a lake — these stretch the mind and lift the spirit of the visitor.

A night in the mountains stays in one's mind. The traveler lies in his sleeping bag, and the stars dance bright overhead, and he may hear the cry of a coyote or the tinkle of the bell around the bell mare's neck. But these punctuate and enhance the over-all and solemn silence, and a man wonders about himself and his place in life and the places and purposes of others in it, and he imagines in a glad moment that he is on to the secret of human life and the life of the planet, or almost on it ... almost ... almost.

And his mind sees the flowers his eyes have seen, the gorgeous flowers, the white blaze of beargrass, and the mysteries of color and shape, and these go along with his almost knowing. If he doesn't quite get there, he is so close, and sleep comes to him and the ring of the bell to the mare's grazing step.

Looking north along the Scapegoat Wall.   RICK AND SUSIE GRAETZ

Top: Susie Graetz and Pat McGuffin descend Beartop Mountain – the valley of the North Fork of the Sun below.   RICK AND SUSIE GRAETZ
Bottom: Looking east at Big River Meadows and Gateway Pass.   RICK AND SUSIE GRAETZ

Top: The Flathead Alps. RICK AND SUSIE GRAETZ
Bottom: The Patrol Mountain area looking down toward Benchmark. RICK AND SUSIE GRAETZ

Top: Again – Beargrass and the Trilobite Range.   RICK AND SUSIE GRAETZ
Bottom: The Swan Crest from the west – the western boundary of the Bob Marshall country.   RICK AND SUSIE GRAETZ

Top: Looking at the North Wall and the Three Sisters – Chinese Wall in the distance.
RICK AND SUSIE GRAETZ
Bottom: Pentagon Mountain and Dean Lake. RICK AND SUSIE GRAETZ

157

Top: The Middle Fork of the Flathead.   RICK AND SUSIE GRAETZ
Bottom: From above Damnation Creek, the South Fork of the Flathead Valley.
RICK AND SUSIE GRAETZ

Top: *Route Creek Pass and Old Baldy.*   RICK AND SUSIE GRAETZ
Bottom: *Headquarters Pass and Rocky Mountain Peak.*   RICK AND SUSIE GRAETZ

Bear Lake and the ridge between Prairie Reef and Slategoat Mountain – the Chinese Wall in the distance.   RICK AND SUSIE GRAETZ